Ralston Crawford

This exhibition is supported by grants from Champion International Corporation and the National Endowment for the Arts, a Federal agency.

Library of Congress Cataloging in Publication Data

Haskell, Barbara.
  Ralston Crawford.
  Catalogue for an exhibition, held Oct. 3, 1985–Feb. 2, 1986.
  Bibliography: p.
  1. Crawford, Ralston, 1906– —Exhibitions.
I. Crawford, Ralston, 1906-. II. Whitney Museum
of American Art. III. Title.
N6537.C734A4 1985 760'.092'4 85-11570
ISBN 0-87427-007-3

Copyright © 1985
Whitney Museum of American Art
945 Madison Avenue
New York, New York 10021

Dates of the Exhibition:
Whitney Museum of American Art, New York, New York
October 3, 1985–February 2, 1986

The Phillips Collection, Washington, D.C.
April 19–June 1, 1986

Portland Art Museum, Portland, Oregon
July 12–August 31, 1986

Akron Art Museum, Akron, Ohio
September 18–November 2, 1986

Cover illustration:
Lights in an Aircraft Plant, 1945. Oil on canvas, 30⅜ x 40¼ inches (77.2 x 102.2 cm). National Gallery of Art, Washington, D.C.; Gift of Mr. and Mrs. Burton G. Tremaine.

Ralston Crawford

Barbara Haskell

Whitney Museum of American Art, New York

In Ralston Crawford's work we see images of America that are familiar. We know these factories, bridges, grain elevators, and wharves. They are symbols for the strengths of our country. Yet through his vision and technique, Ralston Crawford has made them unique—uniquely his and uniquely our own. We at Champion are exceedingly pleased to have been able to help present the work of this great American artist.

Andrew C. Sigler, *Chairman and Chief Executive Officer*
Champion International Corporation

Contents

Acknowledgments

In preparing this study of Ralston Crawford's life and artistic development, I have had essential support and cooperation from the Crawford family. Crawford's widow, Peggy Frank Crawford, spent countless hours reminiscing with me about Crawford and graciously allowed me access to the letters the artist wrote to her throughout their marriage. I am equally indebted to Crawford's sons, Robert, Neelon, and John, who not only shared their recollections of their father but unhesitatingly took time from their own work to make the records of the Estate accessible. Without the collaboration of all the Crawfords this study would not have been possible.

The book has benefited enormously from the support of Christopher F. Middendorf, agent for the Crawford Estate, and Robert Miller, dealer for the Estate, and the staff of his gallery, particularly John Cheim.

Special thanks are also due to Richard B. Freeman, Crawford's lifelong friend and advocate. Not only were his earlier publications on Crawford the foundation for the present study, but he, too, shared the letters Crawford wrote to him over the years. Ruth Dwight generously made available extracts of letters and the essay on Crawford written by her husband and close Crawford friend, Edward H. Dwight. Richard Allen, Allan D'Arcangelo, Malcolm Preston, and Kendall Shaw provided written or verbal impressions of Crawford. In addition, other individuals supplied information on Crawford's family and his early life: Edward L. Baldwin; Richard W. Berry; Violette de Mazia; Sylvia Hamerman; Irvin Himmele; Ardie Kelly; Marion Laskey; Edna Lindemann; Lynn Montijo; Martha Oaks; Herman Sass; Blanche Scott; Ethel Scures; Emily and Burton Tremaine; Norma Weart; Sheila Wilson; Karel Yasko; Andrew Zaremba.

Especially appreciated are the assistance and hard work of my immediate staff. Among those who worked with me over the past three years to assemble biographical and bibliographical data are Amy Mizrahi, Nancy Spector, Marni Dreifuss, Judy Hellman, and Elizabeth Geissler. Mary Joan Bono and Ann MacNary made particularly important contributions, as did Deborah Leveton, who assumed a large share of responsibility for organizing loan and photograph requests and resolving outstanding research questions. I am deeply grateful to them and to Susan Cooke, whose contribution has been invaluable. Her collaborative role in all phases of the project and her management of the myriad details involving book and exhibition production went beyond the usual role of assistant: they were essential to the project's realization.

Finally I would like to thank the National Endowment for the Arts and Champion International Corporation, whose commitment to the arts and belief in the significance of Crawford's achievement made this endeavor possible.

Barbara Haskell, *Curator*

Foreword

The Whitney Museum of American Art is pleased to present the first major retrospective since 1958 of the work of Ralston Crawford. Though Crawford's career spanned more than forty years, the public success he enjoyed in the late 1930s and early 1940s diminished after the Second World War with the emergence of Abstract Expressionism. During a time when American art was dominated by non-objective abstraction, Crawford maintained a steadfast commitment to an aesthetic based on recognizable subject matter, with the result that except for a small number of his Precisionist paintings, his achievements as a painter, as well as a photographer and printmaker, were largely overlooked.

The development of Minimalism in the 1960s and the respect for statements based upon economy of expression have their antecedents in the work of a group of artists active in the 1930s who took forms observed primarily in the cityscape and industrial landscape and emphasized their geometric features in a style of representation known as Precisionism. Crawford's sense of design and his ability to reduce visual impressions to elements of form, line, and color – always based upon natural forms – make the recognition of his work a corollary of our current reassessment of Minimalism.

I admired Crawford, the man, because his spirit always seemed associated with the joys of youth, and I hope he would be pleased to be celebrated because of the quality of his vision and his continuing association with new generations of artists.

We are extremely grateful to Champion International Corporation for sponsorship of this exhibition. The association of Champion with the Whitney Museum began with the Winslow Homer exhibition in 1973. This ongoing commitment to American art represents an extraordinary example of corporate support of the arts. In addition to sponsoring a number of major exhibitions, including "Calder's Universe" in 1976, Champion was the first corporation to host a Whitney Museum branch, the Whitney Museum of American Art, Fairfield County, located in Champion's headquarters in Stamford, Connecticut.

We also extend our thanks to the National Endowment for the Arts, now celebrating its twentieth anniversary, for providing a generous grant for the exhibition. This federal agency has consistently supported programs devoted to expanding public knowledge and understanding American art, and has maintained a particularly strong commitment to living artists.

We appreciate the cooperation of the lenders to the exhibition who have recognized the accomplishment of the artist and now share the work of Ralston Crawford with old friends and new.

Tom Armstrong, *Director*

Ralston Crawford, 1963. Photograph by David Lowell. Ralston Crawford Estate, New York.

Ralston Crawford

Ralston Crawford remains an elusive, if not enigmatic, figure in the history of twentieth-century American painting. It is not uncommon for him to be remembered exclusively for one moment in his career – his crisp, sharp-edged depictions of the American industrial landscape from the late 1930s. And indeed, when *Overseas Highway* (Fig. 51) was completed in 1939, it immediately achieved the status of a national icon, an optimistic affirmation of the industrial future. Crawford became one of the young stars of the art world. The emergence of Abstract Expressionism in the late 1940s dramatically lowered Crawford's status. At the same time, his own work was changing: his diminished faith in the unqualified benefits of industrial progress, precipitated by the war, joined with an increasingly abstract, but hard-edge, approach to painting. The effect was to isolate him further from the audience which had earlier applauded him. Yet Crawford tenaciously adhered to his own aesthetic vision, undeterred by the lack of critical interest. Ironically, his post-1939 work, though less ingratiating and immediately accessible, is perhaps his best and most original. In pursuing a geometric abstraction which was both expressive and rational he sustained an important current in twentieth-century American modernism. Few artists in this century have explored an unpopular style with such commitment and integrity, or have been as successful in producing so powerful and versatile an oeuvre.

George Ralston Crawford was born on September 25, 1906, in Saint Catharines, Ontario, the only son of a ship captain.[1] Both Crawford's father and maternal uncle captained cargo vessels transporting wheat and coal to ports along the Great Lakes.[2] Crawford spent his first four years in Port Dalhousie, on the southern shore of Lake Ontario, which then served as the entrance to the Welland Canals connecting Lake Ontario with Lake Erie; his early memories were permeated with images of shipyards, dry docks, grain elevators, and the austere expansiveness of lakes. Crawford later reflected on "how deeply the vital and most vividly recalled experience is identified with these lakes, these boats."[3] Even the Crawfords' 1910 move to Buffalo did not lessen his affection for ships and harbors, for Buffalo was likewise a port town dominated by the maritime industry.[4] Moreover, every summer the family returned to the waterfront home of Crawford's grandmother in Port Dalhousie, where Crawford would often accompany his father on trips up the Great Lakes.

The family's connection with shipping was severed in 1917-18 when *The Northern Queen*, the vessel Crawford's father sailed, was purchased for the war effort and for some reason he was not reassigned to another boat, a situation he curiously blamed on the Catholics.[5] For the next twenty years, until his death in 1937, he worked as an insurance and real estate salesman in Buffalo. Never able to match his earlier success, his self-image remained fixed on sailing, and Ralston Crawford always spoke of his father as a seaman.

Despite the father's change of profession, the Crawfords seem to have fared well enough financially until the Depression for Crawford to attend Lafayette High School in the upper-middle-class section of Buffalo. During his years there, 1920-26, he was apparently convinced by a number of his art teachers and his winning of several poster competitions that his aptitude lay in the arts (Fig. 1). With the methodical tenacity that would mark all his later professional efforts, he chose to remain an extra two years at the school for "post-graduate" work in the art department. Whether, in fact, these extra years were elective is unclear; although Crawford later described himself as graduating "with honors" and some students did continue at Lafayette for course work after completing their four-year program, the records show Crawford having graduated 279th out of a class of 289 – an indication that scholastic achievement was not then his forte.[6]

Crawford had intended to enter Pratt Institute in New York after graduation in order to further his study of commercial illustration, but he apparently applied too late and the classes were full. He decided to go to New York anyway and get a job as a seaman (during high school he had a job cleaning out dust from the holds of coal barges to prepare them for carrying grain). Arriving in New York with two dollars in his pocket, he immediately hired on with the United Fruit Company ship *La Perla,* which sailed down the East Coast to the banana-producing countries of Guatemala, Honduras, Costa Rica, Panama, and Colombia.[7]

The solitude of the sea and what Crawford described as the "intensely human character of many of the situations" on board ship instilled in him a profound feeling of contact with forces larger than himself.[8] As he would later remark, the "ocean is simply *better* than mountains or a desert or these other fine things that feed the soul."[9] He particularly identified with the description of the dawn watch in Eugene O'Neill's *Long Day's Journey Into Night:*

> Then another time, on the American Line, when I was lookout on the
> crow's nest in the dawn watch. A calm sea, that time. Only a lazy
> ground swell and a slow drowsy roll of the ship. The passengers asleep
> and none of the crew in sight. No sound of man. Black smoke pouring
> from the funnels behind and beneath me. Dreaming, not keeping lookout,
> feeling alone, and above, and apart, watching the dawn creep like a
> painted dream over the sky and sea which slept together. Then the
> moment of ecstatic freedom came. The peace, the end of the quest, the
> last harbor, the joy of belonging to a fulfillment beyond men's lousy,
> pitiful, greedy fears and hopes and dreams![10]

In terms of art, Crawford's six months at sea proved seminal. Although his knowledge of the art profession was still limited to commercial endeavors, his transcendent experiences at sea mitigated his interest in the exclusively lucrative

1. Ralston Crawford (standing, far right) with poster competition prizewinners from Lafayette High School. Photograph from *The Oracle* (Lafayette High School yearbook), 1924.

aspects of art. He decided to study at the Otis Art Institute in Los Angeles and took advantage of the United Fruit Company's new service of transporting fruit from the west coast of Panama to Los Angeles and San Francisco. By securing passage on *La Perla* when it sailed through the Panama Canal en route to Los Angeles, Crawford was able to arrive in Los Angeles in time to attend the winter and spring terms of 1927 at the Otis Art Institute.

Crawford's decision to attend Otis was probably motivated less by the school's curriculum and reputation than by its willingness to accept his late application and its proximity to his sister Jessie, whose residence in Los Angeles provided him with free room and board. Even so, Crawford must have felt the need for supplementary income, for the records indicate that he spent a few days working part-time at Walt Disney Studios painting cels for *Oswald the Lucky Rabbit,* Disney's first complete animation film, then in its initial stages of production.[11] That this short-term employment loomed large enough in Crawford's memory to appear in virtually all of the published chronologies he helped compile suggests that it affected him more profoundly than the $10.50 he received would otherwise justify. Indeed, he later credited the lack of idealism he encountered there as one of the factors in his eventual decision to shift from commercial to fine art.[12]

Crawford's two terms at Otis seem to have passed with little incident. He had entered the school confident that he possessed an unusual aptitude for art, but knowing little about career possibilities outside of the applied arts. In this regard Otis was a fortunate choice. Founded in 1918, it boasted a strong program in illustration, commercial and costume design, and interior decoration, while also offering courses in painting and sculpture. Crawford later claimed that his encounters with the instructors and students in these latter courses laid the groundwork for his commitment to fine art.[13] By the time he left Otis he was well on his way toward a career as a painter.

This career began in earnest in the fall of 1927 with Crawford's enrollment at The Pennsylvania Academy of the Fine Arts, where he spent the next three and a half years. Already by 1927, the Academy had begun its slide toward conservatism.[14] Arthur B. Carles had been dismissed from the faculty in 1925 and only a handful of teachers remained to uphold the cause of modernism, the foremost of whom were Henry McCarter and Hugh Breckenridge. Somewhat inexplicably, given Crawford's lack of exposure to advanced art, he allied himself with this modernist group within his first year at the Academy. Breckenridge in particular became a beloved mentor whose influence transcended a specific painting style. Through him Crawford came to recognize the value of painting pictures with the "best possible procedures," an objective he felt to be incompatible with commercial art.[15]

Breckenridge, who had taught at the Academy since 1894 and numbered among his former students John Marin, Charles Demuth, and John Sloan, ran a summer school in East Gloucester, Massachusetts, which Crawford began attending after his first year at the Academy. There, students had an opportunity to live and work with Breckenridge in an informal atmosphere (Fig. 2). His pervasive enthusiasm, wit, and tolerance made him a cherished teacher to many.[16] With Crawford, the respect seems to have been reciprocated: during Crawford's second and third years at the summer school, Breckenridge provided him with free tuition and a monitor's "honorarium" for living expenses which Breckenridge apparently paid only to protect Crawford's pride. Breckenridge was also instrumental in getting the Academy to give Crawford free tuition in his third year. In his letter of recommendation, Breckenridge praised what would become the hallmarks of Crawford's adult personality: his earnestness, industriousness, and intelligent, active mind.[17]

As a painter, Breckenridge epitomized the bold colorism that characterized the Philadelphia School. During Crawford's student years, he was occupied with his Abstractions series – spontaneous and rapidly brushed works reminiscent of Kandinsky's Improvisations, in which color and the materiality of paint were emphatically elevated above structure (Fig. 3). Although Breckenridge did not impose his own aesthetic preferences on his students, his passion for color was evident in his teaching; indeed, the subheading of his summer school brochure promised the "scientific analysis of color for the artist."[18]

Crawford did not adopt Breckenridge's style, but he wholeheartedly embraced his mentor's conception of what it meant to be an artist. Breckenridge believed that art was a special pursuit demanding an almost obsessional commitment; it was not an activity in which interest in fame or financial reward had a place. Throughout his life Crawford remained fond of quoting Breckenridge's admonition that if there were anything other than art you could do with your life, you should do it.[19] Such idealism would become an essential ballast for Crawford beginning in the late forties when his unswerving insistence on his own aesthetic vision engendered a serious diminution of his income and critical approbation.

Another Breckenridge legacy was a fundamental mistrust of those whose livelihoods linked art and money. For Breckenridge this entailed little hardship; although he never had a dealer, he lived in an era when artists could attain prominence solely through the support of museums and art clubs. By Crawford's time the situation had changed drastically and an artist who was not promoted by a dealer was likely to remain severely underappreciated. Nonetheless, Breckenridge's attitude impressed Crawford, who retained a lifelong wariness of

2. Hugh H. Breckenridge (standing by far wall) conducting a review session of students' work in his studio at The Breckenridge School of Painting, East Gloucester, Massachusetts, 1922.

3. Hugh H. Breckenridge, *Kaleidoscope*, 1927. Oil on canvas, 17 x 21 inches (43.2 x 53.3 cm). Judith Goffman Fine Art, Ft. Washington, Pennsylvania.

dealers — a position which may explain why he never established a long-term relationship with the galleries that handled his work.

More pictorially significant for Crawford was Breckenridge's insistence on a balance between intelligence and emotion. Breckenridge felt that the impulse to paint began with emotion, but that its final expression in art was an intellectual performance. Although an artist strove to generate an emotional reaction in his audience, "feeling and working were not the same thing." "One without the other won't get you anywhere."[20] These notions hit a particularly responsive chord in Crawford, whose father's advocacy of sobriety and emotional restraint had over-ridden his mother's sentimental impulses.[21] This dichotomy would mark even Crawford's friendships, which were often with intense and deeply expressive people – until the manifestation of these very characteristics would make him uncomfortable.[22] In a veiled allusion to his own occasionally volatile temper, Crawford later joked that his ancestors, the Scots, had been so unruly that the Romans were forced to build walls around them to keep them contained.[23] It was almost as if Crawford's lifelong obsession with control was the result of some fear that his emotional side would momentarily erupt and betray him. He even explained his art in these terms: "I suppose one of the reasons for the severity of some of my paintings," he later remarked, "is that I am in many respects an incurable romantic. . . . I am long on feeling, and a lot of discipline – or steering of that feeling – is necessary."[24]

During Crawford's student years, Philadelphia remained relatively inhospitable to modern art. The Pennsylvania Academy had virtually abdicated responsibility for presenting exhibitions of advanced art. One of its last attempts was the 1923 exhibition of seventy-five works from the collection of Dr. Albert C. Barnes, which was greeted with such derision and abuse that Barnes vowed thereafter to make his collection publicly inaccessible. The city's other major institution, the Philadelphia Museum of Art, offered slightly better fare after its facilities were expanded in the spring of 1928, but the museum's policies remained essentially conservative, and its encouragement of the new was marginal.

Yet while Philadelphia's acceptance of contemporary art was limited, the city was far from being a cultural desert. It contained enough individuals interested in modern art to form a lively, though small, alliance in which Breckenridge and McCarter, along with their former Academy colleague Carles, were natural participants. The social ties occasioned by this self-protective group allowed Crawford, as one of Breckenridge's favored students, an extended introduction to modern art – a situation that differed markedly from earlier American modernists who had forged their vocabularies with only limited contact with the developments taking place in Europe.

One focal point for Philadelphia's modern art enthusiasts was the collection of Earl Horter.[25] An artist himself, Horter had made enough money in advertising to have assembled an impressive assortment of twentieth-century art, including twenty-two Picassos and works by Matisse, Braque, and Brancusi, among others; the collection thus provided Crawford with an in-depth contact with Cubism. It also gave him his first view of the work of the Pennsylvanians Charles Demuth and Charles Sheeler. Among the several Sheelers Horter owned was *Church Street El,* whose architectural subject matter, flat planes of color, and smooth paint handling could well have influenced Crawford's later pictorial choices (Fig. 4). In addition to the Horter collection, two other private collections in Philadelphia offered the young Crawford fine examples of vanguard art: that of Samuel and Vera White and that of Mr. and Mrs. Maurice Speiser. The Whites' collection, which Crawford could have seen at their home or at the exhibition inaugurating the expansion of the Philadelphia Museum, included works by the

American modernists Marin and Demuth, as well as those by Matisse, Cézanne, Picasso, Braque, and Rouault, many of which were purchased from the John Quinn estate (as was also true of works owned by Horter). The Speiser collection offered a more eclectic and ultimately modest compilation, but its holdings of over fifty French, Russian, and American modernist pictures buttressed the view of art Crawford obtained from the other two collections.[26]

Through these individuals, Crawford became aware of Dr. Barnes, whose collection of more than seven hundred Post-Impressionist works was the largest and most comprehensive in the country. But Barnes was more than an astute accumulator. Wishing to establish an educational institution from which to disseminate his ideas about art, he had opened the Barnes Foundation in 1924 on his property in Merion, Pennsylvania, on the outskirts of Philadelphia. Here, through seminars, lectures, and classroom demonstrations, students were taught to ana-

4. Charles Sheeler, *Church Street El*, 1920. Oil on canvas, 16⅛ x 19⅛ inches (41 x 48.6 cm). The Cleveland Museum of Art; Mr. and Mrs. William H. Marlatt Fund.

lyze the art of the past and present in terms of objective standards of "plastic form."[27] Underlying all great art, Barnes felt, was the harmonious synthesis of its formal elements — line, color, and space. While no doubt opinionated, Barnes was far from being a *poseur*. He was one of the few champions of formal analysis in an age when American criticism was generally oriented to content and subjective interpretation. For Crawford, who attended lectures at the Foundation — once a week during his second year at the Academy and twice weekly during his third — Barnes' ideas proved liberating. Barnes' analytic approach to art appealed to

Crawford's inherent desire for rational order and helped convince him of the primacy of formal relationships over subject matter or impressive paint handling. Eventually, Barnes' belief that the subject of a painting had no bearing on its quality would free Crawford to create works far less dependent on thematic content than those of many of his contemporaries.

Barnes' establishment of universal standards against which to measure the quality of all paintings gave intellectual credence to Crawford's admiration for the art of the past. Since Barnes' standards applied to all art, being "advanced" held no more favor in his system than did subject matter; hence many of the examples he selected for analysis were historical. In fact, he often compared and contrasted art from different epochs in order to reveal underlying formal properties. Although such an approach may not have been directly responsible for Crawford's appreciation of earlier masters, it certainly encouraged his enthusiasms.

Moreover, Barnes' contention that artists evolved their styles by assimilating the methods of others supported Crawford's later dismissal of originality as a virtue. True individuality, especially for the beginning artist, Crawford maintained, resided in the ability to learn from the work of other artists. "Historical references to the works of previous painters do play a role in the practice of art," he argued. "I consider indebtedness to other artists highly desirable."[28] To be successful, Crawford insisted, the artist must integrate his individual temperament with the whole of his life's experiences — an important part of which were the pictures he saw by other artists.[29]

While Barnes' teaching profoundly affected Crawford's outlook, it was the actual works in his collection that truly emancipated the young student. At the time Barnes opened his Foundation he possessed over one hundred Renoirs, fifty Cézannes, twenty-five Picassos, twelve Matisses, numerous Gauguins and Van Goghs, and other works by a broad range of American and European modernists. Despite Barnes' formalist orientation, he dismissed non-objective art as mere decoration, with the result that few of his works veered toward total abstraction; even the Picassos were drawn primarily from the artist's pre-Cubist period.

Of all Barnes' artists, it was Cézanne who stood as "a mountain in [Crawford's] young life."[30] Crawford recalled being mesmerized for hours in front of Cézanne's paintings, seeing in them the kind of control and solidity he would soon seek in his own work. He admired Cézanne's employment of Impressionist color in the service of structure and his insistence that it function as the building block of form rather than as a decorative appendage. Cézanne's reduction of architectural forms to planes and volumes that achieved unity and rhythm through the repetition, variation, and balancing of analogous forms in various parts of the painting was a revelation to Crawford. In his own early work, he emulated Cézanne's compressed space and his reconciliation of three-dimensional form with the two-dimensional space of the picture plane. Once adopted, these lessons would become the cornerstone of Crawford's aesthetic for the rest of his career.

5. *Untitled (Still Life with Fruit and Coffee Pot)*, c. 1929–30. Oil on canvas, 20¼ x 23 inches (51.4 x 58.4 cm). Ralston Crawford Estate, New York.

6. *Untitled (Portrait)*, 1929. Oil on board, 12⅝ x 11 inches (32.1 x 27.9 cm). Ralston Crawford Estate, New York.

Crawford began the first stage of his Cézanne apprenticeship with a series of still lifes that duplicated the French master's subject matter and his rendering of individual formal elements as solid, three-dimensional entities (Fig. 5). Apart from highly mottled paint, which reflected the influence of Breckenridge, these compositions are pure Cézanne – from their palette to their deployment and handling of forms. Yet, this adulation of Cézanne did not extend as conclusively to Crawford's concurrent portraits and reclining nudes (Figs. 6,7). Rendered with fairly traditional modeling techniques, these figure studies are best seen as the classroom exercises of an inquisitive and earnest student attempting to master the lessons of his instructors.

Gradually, the appeal of Cézanne's structural concerns prompted a dissatisfaction with Breckenridge and his emphasis on color, and Crawford decided to leave the Academy at the end of the 1930 term. By January 1931 he had moved to New York. Given the bleak financial condition of the country, it was a difficult time for anyone to establish himself as an artist, and Crawford later spoke of the period as one in which he "almost starved to death."[31] He tried to earn money by giving private painting lessons, but there were few who were even remotely interested. Despite his extreme poverty, Crawford was unwilling to compromise his search for his own aesthetic voice. In this he was supported by certain of his friends from Philadelphia, particularly Robert Gwathmey, who were now also located in New York. Although a high-spirited camaraderie prevailed among them, Crawford acutely felt the loneliness which befalls many a young artist.[32] Within six months, however, he had been recommended as a recipient of a Louis Comfort Tiffany Fellowship.[33] The fellowship provided him with one month's

7. *Untitled (Nude)*, c. 1929–30. Oil on canvas, 24 x 20 inches (61 x 50.8 cm). Ralston Crawford Estate, New York.

free room and board in Oyster Bay, Long Island – enough time to give him a welcome respite from financial worries. The landscapes that emerged from this sojourn display a far greater mastery of paint than did the still lifes and portraits of his student years (Fig. 8). Forms were more compact and distinctly drawn; color areas, while still built up with multiple paint layers, were less heavily mottled. Although these works still pay homage to Cézanne, they eliminated the device of *passage* which Cézanne employed to fuse foreground and background forms, and instead began to treat compositional areas as discrete planar entities. In several of these landscapes, Crawford also introduced the sharply receding perspective that would reappear in his mature work (as in Fig. 51).

Crawford advanced his mode of simplification in the portraits, landscapes, and interiors he executed over the next year and a half (Figs. 9-12). The paint surface remained comparatively heavy and varied and their compositional formats rooted in the work of Picasso, Cézanne, Matisse, and Juan Gris. Several of these paintings were selected in the fall of 1931 for a group exhibition at the Hotel Marguery in New York, along with works by twenty-five other artists. Included were Milton Avery, George Constant, and Charles Pollock, all of whom, like Crawford, were just beginning their careers in New York. Crawford seemed especially fortunate: one of his paintings was purchased the day the show opened and his name was mentioned in *The New York Times* by Edward Alden Jewell for having created "tastefully and solidly constructed landscapes" – not insignificant acclaim for an artist who had been out of art school less than a year.[34]

8. *Cold Spring Harbor,* 1931. Oil on canvas, 26 x 22 inches (66 x 55.9 cm). Ralston Crawford Estate, New York.

9. *Still Life on Dough Table,* 1932. Oil on canvas, 20 x 18 inches (50.8 x 45.7 cm). Ralston Crawford Estate, New York.

10. *Untitled,* c. 1931. Oil on canvas, 25¾ x 29¾ inches (65.4 x 75.6 cm). Ralston Crawford Estate, New York.

11. *Girl on Elevated*, 1931. Oil on canvas, 24 x 16 inches (61 x 40.7 cm). Ralston Crawford Estate, New York.

12. *Untitled*, c. 1931. Oil on board, 14¾ x 18 inches (37.5 x 45.7 cm). Ralston Crawford Estate, New York.

13. *Untitled (Barns)*, c. 1931. Oil on canvas, 29¾ x 36 inches (75.6 x 91.4 cm). Ralston Crawford Estate, New York.

14. *Nantucket Wharf*, 1932. Oil on canvas, 22 x 26 inches (55.9 x 66 cm). Ralston Crawford Estate, New York.

The works to which Jewell referred were probably from a group of Bucks County landscapes in which Crawford depicted the area's ubiquitous barns (Fig. 13). In these paintings, Crawford rendered the space surrounding the barns naturalistically, but allowed the barns to assume a dominant geometric presence. A year later, in his series of Nantucket Wharf paintings, his propensity for architectural forms began to assert itself even more forcefully (Fig. 14). He retained three-dimensional space while simultaneously blocking infinite spatial recession with a curtain of architectural motifs in the background. In addition, these paintings introduce what would become a recurrent theme in Crawford's work – boats and dockside settings.

Some time during this period Crawford met Margaret Stone, a sculpture and poetry graduate from Sarah Lawrence College who came from a wealthy, old-line Delaware family. After a short courtship, the two were married in October 1932. As a wedding present, Stone's father financed a six-month trip to Europe. Rather than take the traditional whirlwind European tour, Crawford's penchant for thoroughness prevailed and the couple spent most of their time in Paris. There, Crawford tried to paint while intermittently attending the Académie Colarossi and the Académie Scandinav. Since he spoke no French, instruction was presumably secondary to his concern for a studio space and an opportunity to draw from the model. Still, he found it almost impossible to work. He did not want to continue painting where he had "left off," but could not evolve a new approach; as a result, he ended up producing little, save for a series of Mallorca houses, painted during a 1932–33 trip (Fig. 15).[35] Too, he was afflicted by what he later described as the partial paralysis that hits many young American painters in Paris. In this respect, Crawford's experience again differed from that of American modernists such as Sheeler, Demuth, Morton Schamberg, and Louis Lozowick, with whom he was often grouped later. This earlier contingent of American expatriates had found in Europe a hospitable, stimulating environment. A general euphoria had pervaded Paris then as an international group of artists joined together in forging a new and revolutionary aesthetic vocabulary. By the time Crawford

15. *Mallorca Houses*, 1932. Oil on canvas, 18½ x 21¼ inches (47 x 55.2 cm). Ralston Crawford Estate, New York.

arrived, the scene had altered radically. There was no salon comparable to Gertrude Stein's to serve as a comforting refuge or entrance point for Americans. Instead, the battle for modernism had long been won and the tightly knit community of artists from what Roger Shattuck called the "banquet years" had dissolved.[36]

The two dominant currents that reigned in Paris in the early 1930s were Surrealism and Purism. Given Crawford's rational bias, Surrealism held little fascination for him. Purism, on the other hand, emerging after the perceived debacle of World War I, proposed a new utopian system based on the rational organization of society. It attracted a host of converts: Cercle et Carré held its first exhibition in 1930; Art Concret was founded in 1930; Abstraction-Création in 1931; and 1932 saw the first Paris exhibition of "1940."[37] With its emphasis on intellectual order and restraint, Purism might have appealed to Crawford if he had been willing to be less methodical about his own aesthetic maturation. Yet his inherent caution prevented a headlong rush into this new style. Temperamentally, he believed in taking risks only after exhaustive investigation. Such an attitude explains his early apprenticeship to Cézanne: since each step had to be taken in turn, he began with what he felt to be the origins of modern art. Nor did Crawford abstain from applying these obsessive rules to the behavior of others. Once, for example, when his son John wanted to make a leather vest, Crawford insisted that he first make the entire vest in corduroy to test the pattern.[38]

From Paris the newlyweds traveled in France, Spain, Italy, and Switzerland. Everywhere they went, Crawford sought out the museums. But unlike Sheeler, who had been taken with the restrained and architectonic art of the early Italian Renaissance during his travels in 1908-9, Crawford was fired with enthusiasm by the Goyas and El Grecos he encountered on his visit to Spain.[39] From one perspective, the sensibilities of both artists would seem to be far removed from Crawford's. That he was attracted to them so fiercely bespeaks his hidden core of romanticism.

The Crawfords returned to New York in April 1933 and settled into an apartment in Greenwich Village. Believing that the possibility for financial support lay in teaching, Crawford enrolled in a summer class at Teachers College, Columbia University.[40] After finishing the course, however, Crawford found himself as bereft of students as before. With his wife pregnant, money became a growing concern. He later reflected back on this period as one in which the thought of getting a part-time job as a necktie salesman seemed attractive and the only reason he did not pursue it was that no such jobs were to be found.[41]

Crawford's plight was shared by millions of Americans who found themselves out of work during the Depression. As the economy worsened and hopes for a quick recovery faded, the federal government assumed a more active employment role. The program of the Civil Works Administration, whose goal was to give jobs to four million Americans, was extended to art with the establishment on December 8, 1933, of the Public Works of Art Project.[42] Juliana Force, director of the Whitney Museum of American Art, was chosen as regional chairman for New York City and given six hundred jobs to dispense. Although the PWAP was ostensibly an employment rather than a relief program, the administrators disagreed about whether merit or need should be the primary criterion of selection. In New York, with its surfeit of artists, such ambiguity bred tremendous resentment.[43] When the program's funds – and its quotas – were reduced in February 1934, a series of protests against Force led her to close the Whitney Museum, where her headquarters were located, for fear of damage to the museum's artworks.

While Crawford did not take part in these demonstrations, his letters and conversations during this period make frequent references to the artist's need for economic security.[44] His specific attitudes toward the PWAP were probably not unlike those expressed in *The New Hope,* the art magazine for which he was commissioned to write articles.[45] In the September 1934 issue, the magazine's editorial, penned by editor Samuel Putnam, one of Crawford's early supporters, railed against the PWAP for not having treated artists fairly or intelligently. Its criticism of the government's policies reflected the frustrated hostility of those who felt excluded from what they viewed as a favored clique.

Crawford's own experience on the PWAP began with his interview on January 11, 1934.[46] The committee's rather astute assessment of his submitted work as being "not very modern nor yet academic" was apparently adequate to qualify him, for he began to work on January 26 at a salary of $34.00 per week, the allotted amount for nearly everyone on the New York City payroll.[47] At the end of the first month he had finished one painting and was at work on his next composition when he received his termination notice, a victim of the program's reduction in funding. With a mixture of anger and supplication, he wrote to Juliana Force asking that his employment be extended until after the completion of his second painting. But the quotas were firmly set and nothing came of his request — a rejection that may have propelled him toward greater political militancy.

For Crawford this militancy remained essentially intellectual. As with many artists during the 1930s, he was intrigued with Marxism's professed support of artistic freedom and its proposals for an economic system that would encourage creative work. These were not capricious desires. During the 1930s, the need for a new base of economic support for artists had reached dramatic proportions. The dealer-museum-patron nexus which had heretofore been counted on to support the arts was no longer capable of doing so and government-sponsored art projects, however valuable, were not only temporary, but inadequate in proportion to the need. Nor were the artists' worries about freedom of expression unfounded. The PWAP had censored seemingly innocuous political references in a number of its projects and Nelson Rockefeller had blatantly destroyed Diego Rivera's murals at Rockefeller Center. Although Crawford would later participate actively in protest groups (see p. 33), in 1934 and 1935 his political awareness was manifested primarily by his enrollment in a course on the "Fundamentals of Marxism" at the New Workers School, and by his subscription to *Art Front,* an activist publication sponsored by the Artists Union.[48]

Notwithstanding his growing political consciousness, Crawford resisted the arguments on the left for an art of social content and favored instead an allegiance with European painting. In doing so he ran counter to the defiantly nationalistic sentiment of the 1930s. Although the call for a strictly nationalist art which had resounded in certain circles during the 1920s had little prestige among the vanguard, it began to capture the imagination of an increasingly large portion of the art community with the onset of the Depression. By 1932 Regionalism and American Scene painting had triumphed. *What* one painted rather than *how* one painted held the upper hand. This tendency was diametrically opposed, of course, to the formalist view Crawford had inherited from Barnes. For Crawford, the artist's handling of compositional elements – the language of painting – constituted the only justifiable basis of evaluation.

While the denunciations of European art by Regionalist spokesmen such as Thomas Hart Benton and Thomas Craven were overly rabid for most artists, there were others who spoke more calmly and persuasively of the artist's need to turn away from European models and develop an independent American expression. This latter view was not without precedent. During the teens and twenties, the appeal for an indigenous American art was being voiced in magazines such as Robert Coady's *The Soil* and William Carlos Williams and Robert McAlmon's *Contact*, a journal that advocated "contact" with an American subject matter and style. Far from being restricted to the arts, these debates were set against the politics of nationalism which dominated the postwar decade. By the 1920s, the isolationist trend had been expressed in the enactment of immigration restriction laws, the defeat of the League of Nations, the "Red scares," and the government's moratorium on naval construction. This political retreat from the international arena in turn fed the desire for an American art – an art developed on American soil and sustained by American subjects.

By the 1930s, even those who, in the previous decade, had remained unconvinced about the viability of American themes to produce great art had modified their stance. The expatriates of the 1920s had returned home, persuaded that Europe offered less than America.[49] As Holger Cahill wrote in 1934, "American art is declaring a moratorium on its debts to Europe, and turning to cultivate its own garden."[50] Even that stalwart proponent of modernism, Alfred Stieglitz, had come to champion an independent American art and had opened his final gallery, An American Place, with the purpose of exhibiting native artists exclusively.

Ralston Crawford remained effectively oblivious to these shifts away from European art models. His 1938 Guggenheim Foundation application reads like a proclamation from an earlier decade: "I am desirous of studying in Europe because I believe that the vital traditions of modern painting have had their development in Europe. I do not believe that a great American painting can appear over night. I do not believe that a consciousness of the potentialities of the American painter is sufficient. I do not believe in national isolation."[51]

Ironically, the European styles of modern art to which Crawford subscribed had become thoroughly assimilated into the fabric of American art by the mid-1930s. Thus, although Crawford in principle was "out of sync" with the nationalistic views of the time, in reality his art – even his Cézannesque structuralism – sat comfortably with that of his contemporaries. Crawford's by now characteristic architectonic structure, as in *New Hope Station* (Fig. 16; reproduced in a 1934 issue of *The New Hope*) was not unlike that of other artists whose work appeared in the same journal. Crawford's subjects also derived from American localities, primarily rural Pennsylvania: in addition to the 1932 *New Hope Station*, the two other Crawford paintings documented in 1934 were of

16. *New Hope Station*, 1932. Oil on canvas, 25 x 30¼ inches (63.5 x 76.8 cm). Ralston Crawford Estate, New York.

17. *Barn, Exton, Pa.*, 1935. Oil on canvas, 16 x 20 inches (40.6 x 50.8 cm). Ralston Crawford Estate, New York.

18. *Portrait (Margaret Stone)*, 1934. Oil on canvas, 36 x 30 inches (91.4 x 76.2 cm). Ralston Crawford Estate, New York.

barns – one reproduced in *The New York Times* in April; the other executed for the PWAP and described by Crawford as "an early American house occupying about one-sixth of the canvas, the rest being fields and trees."[52]

Apart from subject matter, these and other works from 1934 and 1935 verify Crawford's concern for the solidification of forms into planes and cylinders (Figs. 17, 18). They also reveal his penchant for sober monochromes and his technique of modulating brushy, closely valued hues within individual color areas so that each area appeared distinct. In contrast to the European precedent for collapsing spatial depth, Crawford felt little inclination at this point to flatten his images. Instead, he continued to allow an open area of foreground space in his landscapes to distance the central motif from the picture plane, linking the two areas through the device of a path or road. Crawford's growing confidence and mastery led Edward Alden Jewell to publish an affirmative evaluation in 1935: "Ralston Crawford has somewhat altered his method; while his work still appears derivative, he paints with considerable vigor and seems honestly striving for a style of his own."[53] These comments were appropriate to the work of an artist who was well on his way toward a mature style but had not yet moved unequivocally beyond a formative mode.

Interspersed among Crawford's 1934-35 works were isolated paintings which contained the essentials of his mature style. Inexplicably, he chose not to submit any of these stylistically more advanced paintings to the various group exhibitions in which he participated in 1934 and 1935 or to the Guggenheim Foundation, to which he applied yearly for a grant. Nevertheless, in such paintings as *Marine with Island, Vertical Building,* and *Under the Third Avenue El (The Brewery)* (Figs. 19, 20, 24), brushy modulation and the sculptural modeling of details gave way to sharply demarcated, simplified forms and a smooth handling of color which eliminated all traces of the painting process. These pictures are structured out of large, unmodulated color shapes. While the subjects are clearly recognizable, Crawford established a sense of pure abstract structure by severely reducing details and orienting his forms parallel to the picture plane. *Marine with Island* (Fig. 19) also speaks for Crawford's youthful experiences aboard ship, during which he perceived land across the visually unencumbered expanse of the sea. The pictorial translation of solitude in this painting related to Crawford's experience on the dawn watch and became a hallmark of his work in the late 1930s (as in Fig. 51).

Throughout Crawford's 1931-35 residence in New York he had maintained ties with Philadelphia. Many of the subjects of his paintings from the period derived from the Pennsylvania countryside, while the majority of his exhibitions took place in Philadelphia-area galleries. In New Hope, Pennsylvania, the venue for many of his early exhibitions, Crawford found an engaging society of individuals led by Samuel Putnam, the Marxist editor of *The New Hope.* With Crawford's marriage to Margaret Stone and the couple's visits to her family in Delaware, his

19. *Marine with Island*, 1934. Oil on canvas, 40 x 32 inches (101.6 x 81.3 cm). Ralston Crawford Estate, New York.

activities extended to Wilmington and Baltimore and ultimately led to his first one-man exhibition in 1934 at The Maryland Institute.

In the spring of 1935, Crawford's concern for his wife's health and that of his newborn son precipitated his move to Exton, Pennsylvania.[54] Over the next four years he developed the flat, simplified style with which he would be publicly identified throughout his life. In addition, these years saw the continuation of Crawford's fascination with Surrealism, which had begun in 1934. The incongruous deployment of isolated elements, particularly broken antique statuary, in works such as *Wall with Hand* (Fig. 22), derived from the Surrealist dreamscapes of de Chirico, while in *Coal Elevators* (Fig. 25), Surrealism is responsible for the eerie, forlorn stillness. Crawford's close friendship with the American Surrealist O. Louis Guglielmi during this period would certainly have exposed him to Surrealist theory and practice, but even without Guglielmi he would not

20. *Vertical Building,* 1934. Oil on canvas, 40⅛ x 34⅛ inches (101.9 x 86.7 cm). San Francisco Museum of Modern Art; Arthur W. Barney Bequest Fund Purchase.

22. *Wall with Hand,* 1934. Oil on canvas, 22 x 26 inches (55.9 x 66 cm). Ralston Crawford Estate, New York.

21. *Untitled (Crowninshield Gardens, Delaware),* 1938. Silver gelatin print, 8⅜ x 5¾ inches (21.3 x 14.6 cm). Ralston Crawford Estate, New York.

23. *Columns with Pool,* 1936. Oil on canvas, 30 x 36 inches (76.2 x 91.4 cm). Collection of Mr. and Mrs. Melvin Lenkin.

have been immune to a movement he later acknowledged as being "in the air."[55] Indeed, he felt well enough versed in Surrealism to lecture on it at the Cosmopolitan Club in Philadelphia in 1937. His specific interest in antique statuary and broken columns could have been fueled by the Crowninshield Gardens in Wilmington, Delaware, which he probably saw on one of his visits to his wife's family home in Wilmington. There is no doubt that Crawford found something appealing in the garden's dilapidated classical architecture and statuary, for he painted it several times in 1936 and used it as a photography site after he established a studio in Wilmington following his move to nearby Chadds Ford, Pennsylvania, in 1938 (Figs. 21, 23). Yet the Crowninshield Gardens were not alone in inspiring Crawford, for his wife's sculpted statue fragments and various books on Greek art appear in his photographs of his Exton living room.[56]

When Crawford first moved his family from New York, he had hoped that life in rural Pennsylvania would be less expensive, for his finances remained uncomfortably precarious during this period. Even after the move, he complained of the constant interruptions in his work schedule caused by the need to produce income.[57] His attempt to start a class in painting and drawing met with little success, as did his application for employment in the Works Progress Administration, the successor to the PWAP. That Crawford was rejected by the WPA for failing to meet its relief objectives indicates that his financial situation, however

24. *Under the Third Avenue El (The Brewery)*, 1934. Oil on canvas, 20½ x 16¼ inches (52.1 x 41.3 cm). Private collection.

25. *Coal Elevators*, 1934. Oil on canvas, 20 x 16 inches (50.8 x 40.6 cm). Collection of Wesley Love.

26. *Ventilator with Porthole*, 1935. Oil on canvas, 40 x 35 inches (101.6 x 88.9 cm). Sheldon Memorial Art Gallery, University of Nebraska—Lincoln; F.M. Hall Collection.

marginal he felt it to be, was less severe than that of others. Although he had sold few paintings, he had earned money painting three murals for the Hotel Darling in Wilmington and had presumably received some funds from his wife's family to cover household expenses, perhaps in exchange for the mural he executed in the Stones' Wilmington home. By late 1936, even Crawford acknowledged that his financial success was greater than in the past, although, with the arrival of his second child in September 1936, he considered it less than sufficient to cover the family's living expenses.[58]

By 1936 Crawford had become sufficiently concerned with the artist's place in the economic structure to take a more active part in protest efforts. In February 1936 he attended the first American Artists Congress in New York.[59] The appeal for such a meeting had been issued in *Art Front* over the signatures of 114 artists, a number of whom subsequently became Crawford's close friends: Stuart Davis, future Congress secretary; Niles Spencer; and Joe Jones, future Congress vice president.[60] For three days, 360 delegates listened to speakers address issues ranging from the destruction of democratic liberties and free art expression to the failure of private patronage and the threat of discontinuance of the federal art projects. These concerns mirrored Crawford's own, as did the Congress' more generic opposition to war and fascism. His commitment to the organization was sufficient to warrant his participation in several exhibitions of the American Artists Congress and Artists Union in New York and Philadelphia, and to teach at the Artists Union School in Philadelphia.[61] Prior to the second gathering of the American Artists Congress in December 1937, he wrote to National Executive Committee member Louis Lozowick suggesting that one of the sessions include a discussion of the artist and his audience.[62] His letter addressed the need to establish a functional relationship between artist and worker and prophesied that the support of organized labor would be essential if the Congress were to be effective in its struggle for democracy and peace. This strategy of class alliance echoed that voiced by the American Communist Party. Although Crawford was not a Party member, his letter to Lozowick clearly indicated that he considered himself a Marxist, even to the extent of closing with the ritual sign-off, "Fraternally yours."

Crawford's affiliation with the American Artists Congress remained intact throughout the controversy surrounding the Moscow trials of 1936-38. Crawford aligned himself with those who maintained that evaluating the trials was impossible for anyone outside the Soviet Union. At least 150 artists agreed with this assessment by signing a letter which was published in *The New Masses* in May 1938 in support of the verdicts issued at the trials. Among those signing were Crawford's friends Stuart Davis and Joe Jones, and a "Bruce Crawford," for whom no records can be found. The name may be coincidental, but it is more likely, given Crawford's friendship with Davis and Jones, that he was one of the letter's signatories and that it was a lapse in concentration by a late-night typesetter which transformed his first name into Bruce.

27. *Electrification #2*, 1936. Oil on canvas, 36 x 30 inches (91.4 x 76.2 cm). Private collection.

28. *Steel Foundry, Coatesville, Pa.*, 1936–37. Oil on canvas, 32 x 40 inches (81.3 x 101.6 cm). Whitney Museum of American Art, New York   37.10.

The trials divided the American left, but it was the Russo-German non-aggression pact of August 1939 and the Soviet Union's invasion of Finland in December 1939 that decimated its previous semblance of unity. Outraged by these events, dissatisfied members of the American Artists Congress, led by Meyer Schapiro, lobbied for a vote to censure the Soviet Union. When, instead, the American Artists Congress approved a report essentially exonerating the Soviet Union, approximately thirty members resigned, among them Davis and Crawford.[63] Nevertheless, it was not until 1945, when Crawford read Arthur Koestler's *The Yogi and the Commissar,* that he felt he had finally "closed the case" for himself on communism.[64]

Always outspoken on behalf of his beliefs, Crawford ran headlong into confrontation with the politically conservative sympathies of his banker father-in-law. For Crawford's wife, Margaret, the clash must have been particularly difficult. Although she relished the sense of rebellion which her marriage to Crawford provided, the conflict between his beliefs and those by which she had been raised undoubtedly helped sow the seeds of future discord. Yet Crawford's flirtation with left-wing theory never extended to life styles; indeed, his psychological investment in a patrician posture ran deep. It accounted for his attraction to women from upper-class backgrounds and his retention, even during the Depression, of certain social rituals such as having stationery with his name printed on it.[65] As these preferences became more dominant, they would ultimately distance Crawford from the more aggressively bohemian community that emerged with Abstract Expressionism in the late 1940s.

During Crawford's residency in Exton, he had become associated with the Mellon Gallery on the outskirts of Philadelphia and had developed a friendship with the gallery's director, Philip Boyer. By late 1936, Boyer had opened two gallery spaces – one in Philadelphia and one in New York. He included Crawford's work, along with, among others, that of Arshile Gorky, David Burliuk, Chaim Gross, and Andrew Dasburg, in the group exhibition that inaugurated his New York space in December of that year. Crawford received only scant attention in the press, but his one-man exhibition the following March at Boyer's Philadelphia gallery was greeted with considerable acclaim; indeed, it constituted his "official" entrance into the art world. Accompanied by a brochure with a foreword by Ford Madox Ford, the exhibition included Crawford's stylistically precocious paintings from 1934-35 (Figs. 19, 20, 24, 26) as well as examples of his more mature and confident endeavors (Fig. 28). Crawford's decision to exclude his concurrent but more "backward-looking" figurative works (Fig. 29) resulted in a cohesive modernist statement – one that confirmed the observation made a year earlier by Henry McBride. Reviewing the 1936 Independents show in New York, McBride announced that Crawford and Stuart Davis were "the two best abstract painters" there.[66]

29. *Portrait of John Greiner*, 1937. Oil on canvas, 20 x 16 inches (50.8 x 40.6 cm). Ralston Crawford Estate, New York.

Dominating the works Crawford showed at Boyer's in March 1937 and his one-artist show there that December were paintings of unflinching simplicity from which he had eliminated all extraneous detail in favor of large simple shapes silhouetted against a clear blue sky (Figs. 27, 30–32, 35). Although Crawford pictorially respected cylindrical volumes such as those in *Buffalo Grain Elevators* (Fig. 32), he depicted the majority of his geometric forms as flat shapes. Already in these images of marine apparatus, industrial buildings, and Pennsylvania barns, he displayed his proclivity for treating the different sides of architectural forms as separate planes of color. Smooth, uninflected areas of single hues accentuate the visual interlocking of these flat planes. Within a basic palette of gray, rust-red, brown, and blue, Crawford introduced startling color accents that created rich harmonies of clarity and "infectious gaiety," as Ford Madox Ford remarked.[67] His sharply edged geometric forms, tightly fit together in shallow-spaced compositions, expressed the rigor of structural art while retaining an accessible subject matter distinctly related to the American experience. This union of abstraction and recognizable imagery placed Crawford squarely within the mainstream of early twentieth-century American modernism – a fact not lost on the art community of Chester County, Delaware, which called upon Crawford to defend modern art against the challenge of fellow Chadds Ford resident N. C. Wyeth and his son, Andrew.[68] Yet however abstract the works in Crawford's 1937 exhibitions seemed, by the close of the year they had been superseded by others even less

30. *Ice Plant*, 1937. Oil on canvas, 32 x 40 inches (81.3 x 101.6 cm). Collection of Mr. and Mrs. James A. Fisher.

31. *Theatre Roof*, 1937. Oil on canvas, 32⅛ x 40 inches
(81.6 x 101.6 cm). The Baltimore Museum of Art;
W. Clagett Emory Bequest Fund in memory of his parents,
William H. Emory and Martha B. Emory; and Edward J.
Gallagher, Jr. Bequest Fund, in memory of his son, Edward
Joseph Gallagher III.

32. *Buffalo Grain Elevators*, 1937. Oil on canvas, 40¼ x 50¼ inches (102.2 x 127.6 cm). National Museum of
American Art, Smithsonian Institution, Washington, D.C.

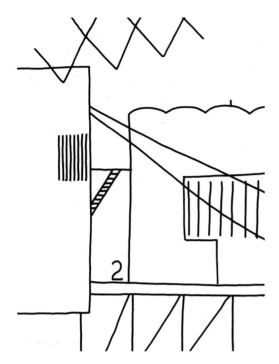

33. *Grain Elevators*, c. 1948. Ink on paper, 14½ x 11⅝ inches (36.8 x 29.5 cm). Ralston Crawford Estate, New York.

34. *Steel Foundry, Coatesville*, 1937. Oil on canvas, 24 x 30 inches (61 x 76.2 cm). Collection of Joseph Helman.

descriptive and detailed. The smaller, 1937 rendition of *Steel Foundry, Coatesville, Pa.*(Fig. 34) eliminated the external accessories of the building which were present in the 1936-37 painting (Fig. 28). It was these more severely reductive statements that Crawford would pursue in the coming years (Figs. 36, 37).

In January 1938, Crawford was one of five artists invited to spend the winter months at the Research Studio in Maitland, Florida, as an artist-in-residence.[69] The program, funded by Mary Bok and inaugurated that year, was the inspiration and life's work of André Smith. An artist himself, Smith had selected the first group of fellowship recipients because they were "men of promise" who had "so far given but little actual evidence of serious accomplishment" – a rather condescending and potentially explosive attitude to hold toward artists who viewed their own achievements quite differently.[70] Smith's knowledge of the fellowship artists was, in several cases, limited: Crawford was chosen after Smith saw his work at Boyer's gallery in Philadelphia, but the later decision to include A. L. Chanin, a staunch Social Realist, was based primarily on Crawford's recommendation.

Personality difficulties beset the program almost from the moment the artists arrived. Abetted by Crawford, Chanin immediately began organizing the artists to demand a stipend for materials and miscellaneous living expenses in addition to the studio space and communal meals provided.[71] Although the protests echoed the debates taking place in left-wing art circles around the country, the

35. *Pennsylvania Barn,* 1937. Oil on canvas, 30 x 36 inches (76.2 x 91.4 cm). Brown Group, Inc., Saint Louis.

36. *Watertank*, 1938. Oil on canvas, 30 x 36 inches (76.2 x 91.4 cm). The Regis Collection, Minneapolis.

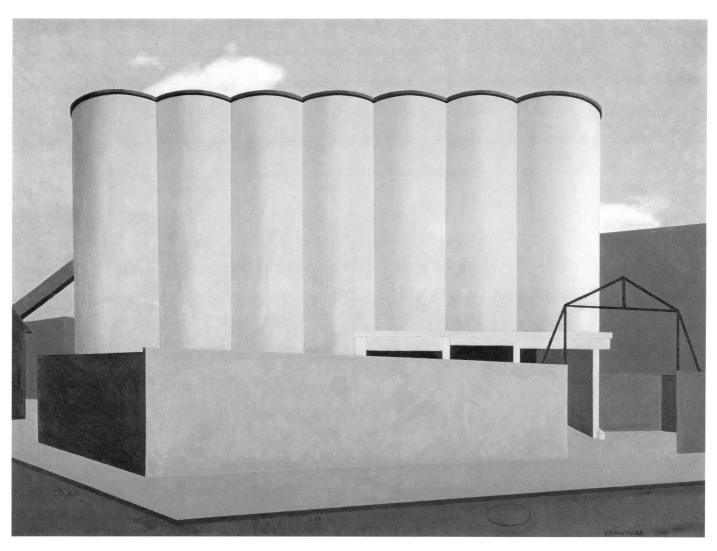

37. *Coal Elevators,* 1938. Oil on canvas, 36¼ x 50¼ inches (92.1 x 127.6 cm). The Saint Louis Art Museum; Gift of Mr. and Mrs. Richard T. Fisher.

38. *Mobile*, 1938. Silver gelatin print, 6⅞ x 4½ inches (17.5 x 11.4 cm). Ralston Crawford Estate, New York.

39. *Orlando, Florida, Prison Camp*, 1938. Silver gelatin print, 6⅝ x 9½ inches (16.8 x 24.1 cm). Ralston Crawford Estate, New York.

application of accusatory rhetoric to the Research Studio seems, on the surface, fairly capricious. Indeed, economic issues may have served as a front for more basic, and finally, more unnerving disagreements over artistic freedom and professionalism. In his year-end report to the Research Studio board, Smith spoke of the artists' dissatisfaction with the staff's "supervision" and recommended that henceforth the Studio select artists more sympathetic to "divid[ing] their time between their own work and the experimental work for which we have organized," the latter presumably being work conceived by Smith for which he needed cooperative artist-assistants.[72] Such an appropriation of artists' time, without financial compensation, would clearly not have been well received by those attending the Studio during its first season. Whatever the cause of unrest, Smith was forced to close the Studio in March, a month earlier than initially intended.

While Crawford's recollections of the Research Studio were far from flattering, the fellowship had enabled him to visit Florida and encounter what proved to be a rich source of new imagery. More important, the trip also occasioned his first experiments with what would become a major tool in his work: photography.

Crawford's initial photographs, taken in 1938, betrayed a fundamental disrespect for the medium. As he later acknowledged, his purchase of a camera was motivated primarily by his recognition that a twentieth-century artist could not avoid an operational knowledge of the device.[73] Not surprisingly, his first photographs, chiefly unposed shots of his family, differed little from the typical amateur or family-album genre. Yet interspersed among them were harbingers of the twin

40. *Ships and Sailors*, 1938. Oil on canvas, 32¼ x 40 inches (81.9 x 101.6 cm). Ralston Crawford Estate, New York.

41. *Untitled (Ships and Sailors)*, c. 1938. Silver gelatin print, 6½ x 9 inches (16.5 x 22.9 cm). Ralston Crawford Estate, New York.

themes that would preoccupy him over the next four decades: images of vernacular American architecture – factories, docks, cemeteries – and documentary pictures of genre subjects. In the latter group are the photos Crawford took of Southern dock workers and the chain gang he observed on his return trip to Pennsylvania (Figs. 38, 39). While these images bear a marked stylistic affinity to the work of Walker Evans, and others employed on the WPA's Farm Security Administration project, they also reflect Crawford's desire for a socially relevant subject matter. The challenge of reconciling revolutionary political positions with the aesthetic discoveries of modernism was one with which many artists on the left wrestled in the 1930s. Crawford's search for a depictive form that would join these seemingly dichotomous goals underlay his 1938 fellowship request to the Guggenheim Foundation to fund a series of canvases on "southern negro life."[74] Though Crawford had retained an interest in portraiture and figurative subjects throughout the thirties, only twice did he introduce images of laborers into large-scale paintings – in *Ships and Sailors,* his entry to the 1939 World's Fair exhibition (Fig. 40), and *Unloading the Cargo.* Both works were based on photographs he took in Florida (Fig. 41).

Architectural images – the other major focus of Crawford's photographic efforts – were likewise initiated on his trip to Florida. The photos he took of this theme in 1938 (Figs. 43, 45, 48) confirm his preference for industrial edifices, but they do not fully exploit the potential for bold abstraction, which Crawford was concurrently investigating in his paintings. Here Crawford differed fundamentally from artist-photographer Charles Sheeler, whose photographs of American architecture anticipated the introduction of similar motifs into his paintings by more than five years.

42. *Sanford Tanks*, 1938. Oil on canvas, 36 x 28 inches (91.4 x 71.1 cm). Collection of Joseph Helman.

43. *Gas Tanks*, 1938. Silver gelatin print, 6 x 4⅜ inches (15.2 x 11.1 cm). Ralston Crawford Estate, New York.

44. *Sanford Tanks #2*, 1939. Oil on canvas, 28 x 36 inches (71.1 x 91.4 cm). Private collection.

45. *Untitled (Maitland Bridge)*, 1938. Four silver gelatin prints, each approximately 2 x 2 inches (5.1 x 5.1). Ralston Crawford Estate, New York.

The paintings Crawford produced after he returned to Wilmington in the summer of 1938 were based largely on photographic records of the South (Figs. 42-48). Indeed, comparing his paintings and photographs reveals an essential aspect of Crawford's genius: an unerring ability to perceive in subjects and situations a formal power which others ignored.[75] For example, from the evidence of Crawford's photographs, Maitland Bridge was a visually undistinguished freeway overpass (Fig. 45). Yet in his various paintings (Fig. 46), his distillations transformed its commonplace structural masses into shapes of awesome monumentality. The process involved no invention, simply a superb attentiveness to the external forms of everyday life.

Crawford's first translations into oil of his Florida experiences, both photographic and mnemonic, show a far greater elimination of detail and expansiveness of forms than in his previous work and a more aggressive cropping of images, so that forms extend to the edges of the canvas rather than being isolated in the center. As in *Sanford Tanks,* space collapses but is not flattened; the play of cylindrical volumes against flat planes generates dramatic spatial tensions (Fig. 42). Perhaps in response to the bright sun of Florida, a pervasive radiance of light permeates these works.

Crawford's expansive, simplified forms were more than a formalist's interpretation of the architectonic shapes of industry. For him, industrial structures were the American counterpart to Europe's Gothic cathedrals.[76] They repre-

46. *Maitland Bridge #2*, 1938. Oil on canvas, 40 x 32 inches (101.6 x 81.3 cm). The Lane Collection.

47. *Public Grain Elevator in New Orleans*, 1938. Oil on canvas, 44 x 34 inches (111.8 x 86.4 cm). Cincinnati Art Museum; Museum Purchase.

48. *Ship at Dock, New Orleans*, 1938. Silver gelatin print, 7 x 4½ inches (17.8 x 11.4 cm). Collection of John C. Waddell.

sented an eminently assured and stable civilization. As he later observed, they were "symbols of the emancipation of the times. They represented the liberation of the world from poverty."[77] The vast, unfettered spaces in paintings such as *Overseas Highway* (Fig. 51) further suggest a sense of optimism and future possibilities.

Crawford shared this exalted vision of industrial civilization with John Marin and Joseph Stella, who had likewise perceived American technology as a metaphor for spiritual transcendence: upon seeing the Brooklyn Bridge, Joseph Stella wrote, "I felt . . . moved as on the threshold of a new religion."[78] But unlike the calm monumentality of Crawford's views, Marin's and Stella's works presented the explosive energy and excitement of the urban metropolis; their paintings exalt motion, change, and speed, all in a fractured style appropriated from European Futurism.

Stylistically, Crawford's work was more appropriately linked with Precisionism, whose architectural subject matter and aesthetic concentration on sharply defined, geometric forms and smooth paint handling mirrored his own pictorial choices.[79] He shared as well Precisionism's insistence on an ordered pictorial discipline and the purging of spontaneity and emotional excess. Just as Sheeler identified his pictures as "attempts to put down the inherent beauty of the subject with as little personal interference as possible,"[80] so Crawford acknowledged that "my own inclination toward classicism disallows the permissibility of disrobing."[81]

Notwithstanding Crawford's stylistic and temperamental alliance with the Precisionists, he was not of their generation. Twenty-three years younger than Sheeler and Demuth, he belonged among the artists who developed Abstract Expressionism.[82] By the time he had finished art school, Precisionism had already been fully launched. By the late 1930s it had become a historical movement, as testified by its inclusion in the landmark exhibition "Three Centuries of American Art," which opened in Paris in 1938, and by Sheeler's retrospective that same year at The Museum of Modern Art. But while Crawford had at some level been absorbing Precisionism since his student visits to Earl Horter's collection in Philadelphia, his appropriation of the architectonic and the structural grew independently out of his study of Cézanne at the Barnes Foundation. Indeed, Crawford did not so much annex the style of the older Precisionists as duplicate the route they had traversed in the early 1920s in creating an accessible version of Synthetic Cubism. Owing perhaps to the later – and more advanced – aesthetic climate in which Crawford matured, his vocabulary was far more aggressively simplified and his forms more broadly handled than those of the other Precisionists. In comparison to Sheeler's *Upper Deck* and Demuth's *Modern Conveniences* (Figs. 49, 50), Crawford's *Sanford Tanks #2* (Fig. 44) reveals a bolder assimilation of the planar structure of Synthetic Cubism.

Crawford's attitude toward the American industrial landscape likewise differed from that of the majority of Precisionists, who saw it primarily as a vehicle for uniting recognizable subject matter with the abstract forms and flattened space of Cubism. For them, the social ramifications of technological innovations

49. Charles Sheeler, *Upper Deck,* 1929. Oil on canvas, 29⅛ x 22⅛ inches (74 x 56.2 cm). Fogg Art Museum, Harvard University, Cambridge, Massachusetts; Purchase, Louise E. Bettens Fund.

50. Charles Demuth, *Modern Conveniences,* 1921. Oil on canvas, 25¼ x 21⅜ inches (65.4 x 54.3 cm). Columbus Museum of Art, Ohio; Gift of Ferdinand Howald.

were less interesting than technology's clean lines, angular shapes, and smooth surfaces. As Sheeler remarked about his painting, "It's purely a visual thing. . . . [There are] no overtones of symbolism."[83] Crawford followed Sheeler in upholding the primacy of the visual: "A painting is a thing *seen*," he wrote in 1939. "It is not something to be *read*. . . . I want to remember content, but also to remember that I am speaking the language of a painter."[84] Yet at the same time, painting was not for Crawford a purely objective pursuit. He endowed his canvases with a psychological mystery whose reverberations transcended formalist or thematic interpretations, a quality noted by several of Crawford's contemporaneous commentators, particularly his friend and Boyer colleague David Burliuk.[85]

Crawford's union of the abstract and the psychological was to benefit him when he opened his first New York one-man show in February 1939 at Boyer's gallery. Because his subjects were industrial, they were perceived as distinctly American.[86] His paintings, therefore, despite their modernist vocabulary and intention, managed to skirt the challenge launched against modernism by the Regionalists and Social Realists; they were universally lauded by critics who marveled at their successful compromise between subject matter and abstraction. Other accolades followed. Crawford was chosen to serve on the Pennsylvania artists' selection committee for the New York World's Fair and in February 1939 *Life* magazine featured a color reproduction of *Overseas Highway* in an article on San Francisco's Golden Gate Exposition. The image of a causeway speeding precipitously into space was immediately embraced by a nation emerging from the

51. *Overseas Highway,* 1939. Oil on canvas, 28 x 45 inches (71.1 x 114.3 cm). The Regis Collection, Minneapolis.

doldrums of the Depression. Overnight Crawford became a national celebrity. For him, the popularity of *Overseas Highway* was a mixed blessing: he became so identified with the painting that it was difficult to interest people in his other work, a situation which became more critical as he began to modify his style.

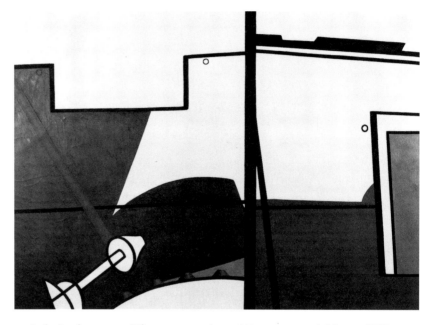

52. *At the Dock #2*, 1941–42. Oil on canvas, 22½ x 15½ inches (57.2 x 39.4 cm). Neuberger Museum, State University of New York at Purchase; Gift of Roy R. Neuberger.

53. *Boiler Syntheses*, 1942. Oil on canvas, 35¼ x 50¼ (89.5 x 127.6 cm). Munson-Williams-Proctor Institute Museum of Art, Utica.

Crawford's public acclaim did little to ease the emotional trauma that he and Margaret experienced as they confronted the painful reality that their eldest son was mentally handicapped. This tragedy seems to have dealt the final blow to the marriage. Even under more bearable circumstances, marriage to Crawford had not been easy for Margaret. Crawford's loyalties, divided between being a traditional provider and being an artist, generated tensions. So, too, did his denigration of sentimentality, an attitude he had learned from his father. As an adult, Crawford spoke proudly of his father's intolerance of his mother's "gushing" and the dismissal of her romantic attitudes as "a lot of rubbish."[87] Though Crawford inherited certain aspects of his mother's romantic character, his self-conscious rejection of it could not have provided much sustenance to a woman like Margaret whose father and older brothers had always coddled her. Despite their fights, however, Crawford was deeply in love with Margaret and the idea of separating from her and accepting the condition of his son hit him with a despair from which he would never fully recover.[88] He later described this period as being the darkest of his life and confided to his son Robert that his depression had been so extreme that on one occasion, while driving in the country with his wife and eldest son, he had desperately wanted to drive the car off a cliff – an impulse he believed explained his subsequent unpleasant association with verdant landscape.[89]

By the late spring of 1939, Crawford had agreed to Margaret's request for a divorce and had moved into the Hotel Brevoort in Greenwich Village. Despite his underlying emotional distress, the period was a socially engaged one for him, marked by political activism and late-night drinking stints with artist friends, among them Stuart Davis and Niles Spencer. It was also a period of economic crisis; though Margaret's parents had assumed financial responsibility for her and the children, Crawford remained without any viable means of supporting himself. Rather than compromise his aesthetic quest by turning out acceptable versions of previously acclaimed paintings, he attempted to find employment in the applied arts. One result was the illustrations he made for the book *Stars: Their Facts and Legends,* published in 1940.[90] Such jobs were of limited supply, however. With little prospect of gallery sales, especially after the closing of the Boyer Gallery in 1940, Crawford decided that teaching would offer the surest means of circumventing a reliance on painting sales and thus ensure his aesthetic freedom – an option which would prove mandatory throughout his life.

54. *Grey Street,* 1940. Silkscreen on paper, 12 x 15 inches (30.5 x 38.1 cm). Ralston Crawford Estate, New York.

The first of Crawford's many teaching stints took him to the Cincinnati Art Academy as a visiting art instructor for the 1940-41 season.[91] Prior to his arrival, he wrote a letter to the head of the Academy in which he listed every major New York art critic and suggested that they would all be interested in knowing of his appointment.[92] Whether Crawford wanted simply to strengthen his standing in the department or was acting out of a somewhat exaggerated image of the job is unclear. Whatever the motivation, the New York art press remained oblivious, while the local newspapers heralded him as an important art world personality. His celebrity status undoubtedly worked in his favor when he met Peggy Frank, the vivacious and attractive co-founder of The Cincinnati Modern Art Society, under whose auspices he exhibited that spring with Sheeler, Demuth, and Spencer in a show of "A New Realism." In Peggy, Crawford found a partner as economically and socially well placed as Margaret had been, but who shared his enthusiasms and was responsive to his needs as an artist; they married in February 1942.

While in Cincinnati, Crawford extended his experimentation with printing techniques by creating a lithograph of *Marine* and silkscreen of *Grey Street* for the Modern Art Society (Fig. 54). His interest in lithography had begun in 1936, when he requested technical information on the medium from the American Artists School in New York.[93] But it was not until 1940 that he engaged the services of printer George Miller to produce his first print, a color lithograph of *Overseas Highway*. Although neither *Overseas Highway* nor *Grey Street* did much more than translate painted images onto paper, both were relatively successful: *Overseas Highway* won a fourth-place purchase prize in The Metropolitan Museum of Art's "Artists for Victory" show in 1942, and both images were widely acquired by public institutions around the country. Ironically, their widespread distribution ultimately worked to Crawford's disadvantage by publicly cementing his identification with the Precisionist style which had launched his career.

Meanwhile, Crawford had begun to move beyond this style. A comparison between *At the Dock #2* (Fig. 52) and an earlier version of the same motif, *Public Grain Elevator in New Orleans* (Fig. 47), reveals how abstract his treatment had become. By 1942 this tendency was even more pronounced as he replaced his earlier inward sweeps of space with radically flattened planes brought close to the picture surface. With the elimination of modeling and perspective, shapes became arrangements of flat color areas. No longer were forms silhouetted against a clear blue sky; they now filled the entire canvas. As with *Grain Elevators from the Bridge* and *Boiler Syntheses* (Figs. 55, 53), Crawford ceased to translate the subject's visual appearance, even if in a simplified, geometric way; rather, he began to distill his experience *about* the subject. Henceforth, his goal in painting would be "selection, elimination, simplification and distortion for the purpose of conveying emotional and intellectual reactions to the thing seen."[94]

These 1942-44 paintings projected the same affirmative view of America as had Crawford's Precisionist paintings. Critics correctly perceived them as embodying a "faith in the final unity of man's genius with the machine" and noted that "his message of optimism . . . makes his art stand out in the era like pillars of fortitude in a morbidly crumbling world."[95] Richard B. Freeman, Crawford's longtime friend and champion, affirmed a similar optimism: Crawford "sees the industrial age . . . as the age when man will free himself by the intelligent use of the machine."[96] That critics saw Crawford's optimism as singular was understandable in the early 1940s, for the Depression had made many

CRAWFORD

55. *Grain Elevators from the Bridge,* 1942. Oil on canvas, 50 x 40 inches (127 x 101.6 cm). Whitney Museum of American Art, New York; Gift of the Friends of the Whitney Museum of American Art   63.22

artists disillusioned with rapid technological development. The turn from utopian celebrations of machine-age America to a didactic Social Realism in the work of Precisionist Louis Lozowick mirrored the cynicism many felt about technological progress. At the same time, the public's belief in technology's achievements and its promise for the future had not dampened. Indeed, throughout the 1930s, the appropriation of geometric or mechanical designs to ornament buildings and functional objects was widespread. Equally well-tuned barometers of public opinion were the 1933 Chicago World's Fair and the 1939 New York World's Fair, both thematically based on the triumph of edified social, economic, and technological engineering.[97] In such a climate, it is no wonder that Crawford's optimistic visualization of machine-age culture found a receptive audience.

Aesthetically as well, Crawford's paintings suited perfectly the tenor of the times. By the early forties the influx of European artists and intellectuals to America had created a situation in which America seemed to be in a position to assume the mantle of international cultural leadership. To fulfill this promise, however, American artists had to devise an art independent of both Parisian modes and of the reactionary nationalist art that had dominated American production for the previous ten years. Exactly what form this new art should take was unclear, but the most plausible answer was a modernist style tinged with American aggression, intensity, and optimism. Such was the argument advanced by Samuel Kootz in his 1941 letter to *The New York Times*.[98] Kootz' letter generated widespread attention and precipitated much of the discussion about the need for an art capable of representing the new America. That Kootz viewed Crawford's work as at least a candidate for this task became clear when he invited Crawford to participate in the exhibition of contemporary American art he organized for Macy's department store in 1942 and by his inclusion of Crawford in his 1943 book, *New Frontiers of American Painting*.

Prior to 1945, the style that seemed on the verge of filling Kootz' prescription was that practiced by geometric abstractionists such as Carl Holty, Ilya Bolotowsky, John Graham, Balcomb Greene, Byron Browne, and George L. K. Morris. Geometric abstraction had been given legitimacy in the late 1930s with the formation of the American Abstract Artists and the New York exhibitions "Cubism and Abstract Art" and "Abstract Painting in America" at The Museum of Modern Art and the Whitney Museum of American Art, respectively. Although Crawford disavowed any connection with the American Abstract Artists as a group, and felt little kinship with either their biomorphic or Neoplastic vocabularies, the hard-edged, abstract mode of his 1942-44 paintings does have a natural affinity with theirs.[99]

But Crawford's insistence on an intuitive relationship to his subject was antithetical to the *a priori* abstraction of the geometric artists. Crawford would simplify, flatten, or distort a motif, but he would never invent imagery; at the core of his approach to painting was the belief that aesthetic quality derived from the artist's emotional contact with the natural world. In this regard he resembled Stuart Davis, who likewise subscribed to abstraction, but believed that artists must begin with nature as their subject. Both Davis and Crawford presumed that social meaning – a vestige from their political days – could be invested in abstraction only through a subjective approach to subject matter, and they consequently distrusted "pure" geometric forms that did not spring from real experience. Crawford wanted no part of an art of "essences" or eternal values. His hierarchical division between geometry and intuitive abstraction accounted for his lifelong contention that his work was not geometric, its outward appearance notwithstanding. "My work is usually charged with emotion, and not of a basically geometric character," he wrote. "I realize this comment is quite at variance with many responses to my pictures, but I am never concerned with a pictorial logic to the exclusion of feeling."[100]

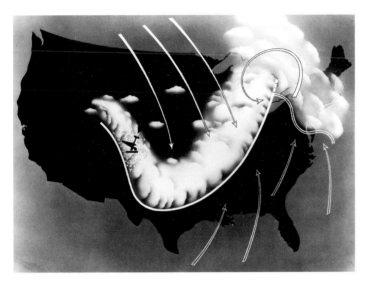

56. *A Plane Accident in Relation to Storm Structure*, 1943. Visual weather presentation for the Army Air Forces Weather Division. Ralston Crawford Estate, New York.

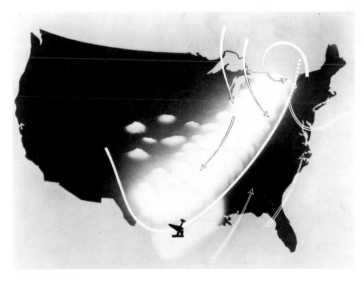

57. *Plane Crash in Relation to Storm*, 1943. Visual weather presentation for the Army Air Forces Weather Division. Ralston Crawford Estate, New York.

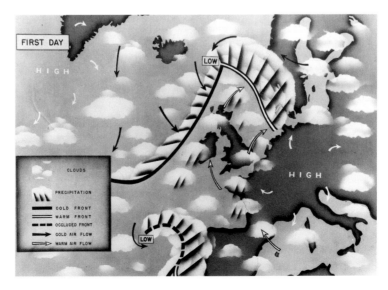

58. *Precipitation Map*, 1943. Visual weather presentation for the Army Air Forces Weather Division. Ralston Crawford Estate, New York.

59. *Bomber*, 1944. Oil on canvas, 28 x 40 inches (71.1 x 101.6 cm). Ralston Crawford Estate, New York.

60. *Air War*, 1944. Oil on canvas, 16 x 22 inches (40.6 x 55.9 cm). Ralston Crawford Estate, New York.

61. *Bomber*, c. 1945. Gouache on board, 10½ x 15¼ inches (26.7 x 38.7 cm). Ralston Crawford Estate, New York.

62. *Aircraft Plant,* 1945. Oil on canvas, 28 x 40 inches (71.1 x 101.6 cm). Cincinnati Art Museum; Gift of Emil Frank.

Crawford's participation in the development of a new American art was effectively halted in February 1942 with the arrival of his draft notice. In contrast to the nascent community of advanced artists in New York whose members, though eligible, generally managed to avoid serving, Crawford's Puritan-derived conviction that "*doing* the thing" occupied a higher moral plane than "getting someone else to do it" kept him from dodging service.[101]

Crawford entered the military aware of its potentially detrimental effect on his career. In a letter requesting deferment until the close of the school term, he prophetically noted that "conditions in the art business are such that if appropriate arrangements for the handling and exhibition of an artist's work are not made, he disappears from the artistic world completely."[102] He later confessed that his induction changed his life dramatically.[103] For a young man in his thirties he had attained remarkable success; he was at this time, as Russell Lynes noted, "one of the bright young stars, a man who already had far more than promise and was bound to have a distinguished future."[104] Crawford's isolation from the art scene and lack of production during the war destroyed this professional momentum. By the time of his discharge, "four precious years [had] passed"[105] – years in which a new generation of artists, with values totally alien to Crawford's, captured the international spotlight.

Crawford had responded to induction by applying for an appointment as a photographer in the Navy. Failing to pass the Navy physical, however, he enlisted in the camouflage division of the Army Engineers' Corps. His six months in basic training at Fort Meade, Maryland, were psychologically disastrous. For him "the enemy was not Hitler, or Mussolini" but what he considered "those miserable, stupid and sometimes vicious people" who conducted the recruits through basic training "in modern assassination techniques." He added that his awareness of destruction as the principal fact of the time had been fertilized by *his* near destruction at Fort Meade.[106] Cut off from art – which provided him with pleasure and psychological balance – and thrown into a depersonalized system that stripped away all remnants of individuality, Crawford felt deracinated and inconsequential. His dream of individual freedom through industrialization and collective action was shattered. Fort Meade forced Crawford to reevaluate his world view. The political and social solutions which, in the thirties, seemed imminent, now seemed impossible to realize. Never again would Crawford be able to view industrial constructions as untarnished symbols of man's potential emancipation.

Anxious to reunite with Peggy after basic training, Crawford lobbied for an assignment which would transfer him to Washington, D.C. In December 1942, through a friend, he procured a job with the Visual Presentation Unit, Weather Division. His task was to translate the meteorological data necessary in planning military operations into a form quickly and accurately comprehensible by Army Air Force personnel.[107] To do this required methods of presentation quite different from conventional charts. Through the use of symbols identified with specific weather conditions – rain, snow, clouds, and fog – Crawford was instrumental in devising a means of pictorializing the weather (Figs. 56–58). Some of his maps described the conditions prevalent during past events, such as a plane crash or bombing mission, while others depicted meteorological forecasts. Such predictions were based not on information about existing weather conditions, but on an analysis of such variables as topography, seasons, pressure centers, and normal air flow of a given region. Though Crawford merely pictorialized the climatologists' information, their technique of drawing analogies between past synoptic situations and future ones would encourage Crawford's postwar pictorial emphasis on the synthesis of remembered and contemporaneous visual stimuli.

During his period of residency in Washington, Crawford's life was relatively civilian in character. Yet painting took more concentration and sustained energy than he could muster, and he found himself stymied in making art. Even his occasional output – for example, *Bomber* and *Airwar* (Figs. 59–61) – possessed a content that depressed him. Based on the plane wreckages he observed on assignment, these works were utterly distinct from his previous style. In place of large, clear-cut shapes, they employed splintered lines and scattered forms with raw, jagged edges to portray disorder and destruction. As Crawford wrote to Richard Freeman: "They are the most solid expression of which I am capable at this time. . . . A more directly constructive expression would lack substance because of my present reactions."[108] In addition, Crawford once again felt financially unable to cover his and Peggy's expenses, with the result that he was constantly lobbying for various promotions; one such bid – albeit unsuccessful – was made through his father-in-law to Senator Robert Taft.[109]

Crawford did try to keep his career from foundering during the war by enlisting the aid of various artists, Stuart Davis among them, to speak on his behalf to Edith Halpert, the owner of the Downtown Gallery.[110] Their efforts proved successful, and Halpert asked Crawford to join her gallery in the spring of 1943. This association placed Crawford in the company of some of the most renowned artists of the day: Sheeler, Davis, Spencer, Guglielmi, and Kuniyoshi, among others. Crawford's first show with the gallery, in January 1944, included a number of his meteorological studies along with fourteen oils executed prior to his induction. The exhibition drew an extremely favorable response from the press, many of whom devoted a significant amount of attention to Crawford's weather maps. This exposure led to a commission from the Miller Lighting Company to make a painting of the new lighting system at the Curtiss Wright aircraft plant in Buffalo (Figs. 62–64), and to an assignment in November 1944 to design a cover for *Fortune* to accompany their article on weather, "Thunder Over the North Atlantic."[111]

Near the close of the war, Crawford received an assignment to inspect, on site, the charts produced at India's various weather stations. He sailed in mid-September, only days before the United States signed the armistice with Japan. Artistically, the trip offered him an opportunity to visit and photograph many Buddhist temples and caves, among them Ajanta and Ellora. Intellectually, it provided him with an opportunity to formulate – and detail to Peggy by letter – an aesthetic

63. *Lights in an Aircraft Plant,* 1945. Oil on canvas, 30⅜ x 40¼ inches (77.2 x 102.2 cm). National Gallery of Art, Washington, D.C.; Gift of Mr. and Mrs. Burton G. Tremaine.

64. *Nacelles Under Construction,* 1946. Oil on canvas, 30 x 36 inches (76.2 x 91.4 cm). U.S. Steel Corporation, Pittsburgh.

credo that joined art with religion.[112] The religious component of the merger had its origin in Crawford's boyhood experiences in the Presbyterian church.[113] He described himself as believing, until the age of twelve or fourteen, in a divine being who judiciously dispensed reward and punishment for good and bad conduct. By adolescence this behavioral model had been internalized into an acceptance of man's social obligation to man. This belief probably had motivated Crawford's involvement in left-wing political organizations, which he had seen as embodying a more ethical way of thinking than that underlying capitalist systems. With the perceived failure of these political experiments Crawford had made art his chosen arena for social contributions. He viewed art as fundamentally ethical in its potential to serve as a model for a rational and ordered society. For him, art's ethical significance was directly proportionate to its elimination of chaos and sentimental caprice: he often measured the value of his work against the civilizing effect it had in stimulating the viewer's "sense of fitness, – the rightness of certain relationships" which were important in all human endeavor.[114] He responded to the horrors of war, for example, with a conviction that he had to do something aesthetically constructive; he wrote to his friend Bill Swing that if his work had even a small positive social direction, it could justify his existence.[115] At the same time, Crawford's equation of the religious and aesthetic allowed him to view works of art as conduits for transporting viewers to non-rational realms in which experience was generated without regard to verifiable externals. Such a reading of aesthetics buttressed his earlier instinct that the purely rational approach was "hopelessly inadequate."[116]

Crawford's first opportunity to manifest this newfound social consciousness occurred in the paintings he executed in conjunction with the atomic bomb detonation in 1946 at Bikini Atoll in the Marshall Islands. The test had grown out of the Navy's concern, following Hiroshima, about the effects of an atomic missile on a warship or fleet.[117] After the war, the Joint Chiefs of Staff decided to perform a test on a dispensable fleet to be anchored in the Bikini Atoll lagoon. Operation Crossroads, as it was called, consisted of two bomb drops: Test Able, the over-water detonation, and Test Baker, the underwater explosion. Although an atomic bomb had been exploded earlier over Nevada, these tests were the first to be treated as "public" events, with over 42,000 military experts, congressmen, scientists, and foreign observers participating. A broad range of news and radio agencies were also invited to send representatives to cover the blast. While all other agencies selected veteran reporters and photographers, *Fortune* selected Crawford, who not only had experience with weather charts, but by this time had illustrated several articles and designed two more covers for the monthly.[118] Thus, of the 124 international and national press representatives who witnessed the test, Crawford was the only artist.

A few seconds after 9:00 a.m. on July 1, 1946, the bomb was dropped. Typically, Crawford had gone out of his way to see as much as possible, negotiating to observe the targeted area prior to the blast and to be on board the S.S. *Appalachian,* which entered the lagoon forty-eight hours later. For many on-site observers, Test Able was something of a disappointment because the damage was far less than expected: of the seventy-three targeted vessels, only three were sunk and eighteen damaged; the Bikini palm trees stood unscathed; the goats on board the warships continued to feed. Moreover, in contrast to its destructive potential, the blast was visually beautiful. Even Crawford noted that it had a "profound majesty," despite the "rotten feeling that we all had as we watched it. . . . "[119]

Aware that the most terrifying aspect of the bomb was unseen, Crawford pressed *Fortune* to focus much of their article on the blast's radioactive after-effects.[120] He worked closely with scientists and meteorologists to assemble information on the radioactive wind currents at Bikini and to predict those which would pertain if the bomb had been dropped on New York City. Crawford's research, his resultant charts, and two of his paintings joined several documentary photographs of the blast in *Fortune*'s December issue on Bikini.

Creating these and other paintings on the theme proved a formidable task for Crawford: "interpretative" abstraction was a greater challenge than direct transcriptions might have been. "It seems I have to coin so many new 'words,' i.e. shapes," he had written from Bikini. "It has never been so difficult."[121] Perhaps because of this, only a few of Crawford's Bikini paintings dealt with the explosion and its attendant wreckage (Figs. 66, 67); the others derived their imagery from

65. *Weather Reconnaisance Plane,* 1946. Oil on canvas, 10¼ x 14 inches (26 x 35.6 cm). Ralston Crawford Estate, New York.

66. *Test Able,* 1946. Oil on canvas, 23⅝ x 17⅝ inches (60 x 44.8 cm). Georgia Museum of Art, The University of Georgia, Athens; Eva Underhill Holbrook Collection of American Art; Gift of Alfred H. Holbrook.

67. *Tour of Inspection, Bikini,* 1946. Oil on canvas, 24 x 34 inches (61 x 86.4 cm). Ralston Crawford Estate, New York.

the flight across the Pacific to the testing site (Fig. 65). Stylistically, this latter group related to Crawford's prewar style (Figs. 53, 55); the former to the work he had executed during the war (Figs. 59–61). In the paintings reflecting Crawford's experience of the explosion, his introduction of the colors surrounding the event – the brilliance of the blast and the red, white, and yellow that were applied to the U.S.S. *Nevada* for greater target visibility – contributed to the sense of ruptured quiet. Here was an art that bespoke a world coming apart, a world whose stability and prewar assurance had been irrevocably lost. The vocabulary of fractured, spiked forms in the Bikini paintings appeared idiosyncratic within Crawford's oeuvre; even he characterized them at the time as important but in the nature of an aside.[122] Yet in later work, Crawford would return to similar motifs to describe wreckage or dilapidation – as in his Cologne and Torn Signs series (Figs. 114, 115, 135, 137, 138).

Eight of Crawford's Bikini paintings and a group of auxiliary gouaches were presented at the Downtown Gallery in December 1946. In the brochure statement accompanying the exhibition, Crawford explained them as comments on the force of destruction rather than as visual illustrations of the blast:

> Destruction is one of the dominant characteristics of our time. These pictures constitute a comment on destruction. They most certainly do not explain the atomic bomb, nor do they give quantitative information about the ships. They refer to these facts. They refer in paint symbols to the blinding light of the blast, to its color, and mostly to its devastating character as I saw it in Bikini Lagoon. However, it is futile to look for illustrative value in each detailed area. My purpose has been to convey ideas and feelings in a formal sequence, and not reproduce nature.[123]

Despite the disclaimer, Crawford's paintings were actually less convincing as psychological representations of the destructive power of the blast than as descriptions – albeit abstract – of its visual effect, which Crawford himself acknowledged as beautiful. Even granting his proclaimed desire to depict the "devastating character" of the event, his paintings highlighted the difficulty of communicating subjective emotions with an abstract vocabulary, especially a geometric one. The generally negative reaction of the press to the series represented Crawford's first fall from critical favor. For many, his rendition of the blast was inappropriate for conveying the vision of a landscape razed by nuclear devastation. Reviewers found in his cool, smooth paint handling a refusal to commit himself emotionally.[124] The critic for the *New York Herald Tribune* characterized his paintings as "betray[ing] startling indifference to the drama of the events depicted," while Ad Reinhardt ended his short appraisal of the show with the hypothetical exchange: "Do crooked shapes and twisted lines represent painting's adjustment to the atomic age? (NO)."[125] The most vitriolic abuse was leveled at Crawford by the left-wing *Daily Worker*, whose reviewer lambasted him for expressive inadequacy and tacitly accused him of conspiring with *Fortune's* publisher, Henry Luce, to avoid any social, political, or human implications of the blast.[126] Iron-

68. *Plane Production*, 1946. Oil on canvas, 28⅛ x 36¼ inches (71.4 x 92.1 cm). Auburn University, Auburn, Alabama, on extended loan to the Montgomery Museum of Fine Arts.

ically, it was probably the artists whose proximity to the bomb was strictly intellectual who were able to incorporate its horror into their work. Indeed, a strong case has been made that the explosion of the atomic bomb at Hiroshima and Nagasaki was a central impetus for the surge of primal, mythic content which appeared in the work of the Abstract Expressionists after 1945.[127] To the public, the Abstract Expressionists' evocation of primordial matter stuggling against nature's wrath to build a new world seemed a more fitting metaphor of the atomic era than did Crawford's more restrained renditions.

Unfortunately for Crawford, the critical disaffection he suffered over his Bikini pictures would not be limited to these works. The following year his art was attacked by members of Congress and the press who were protesting the character of the collection of contemporary American art purchased by the State Department for circulation in Europe and South America.[128] For them, Crawford's art was simply too abstract to be comprehensible. When the Assistant Secretary of State for Public Affairs, William Benton, appeared before the House Appropriations Committee to defend the Department's purchases for "Advancing American Art," a reproduction of Crawford's *Plane Production* (Fig. 68) was among those the committee chairman, Karl Stefan, used to bait Benton:

Stefan [holding up a photograph of *Plane Production*]: Do you know what this is?

Benton: Are you holding it up straight?

Stefan: It is straight. Do you know what it is?

Benton: It does have a resemblance to many things that are not fit to mention before this committee.

Stefan: What would you say that was?

Benton: You are closer to it than I am.

Stefan (moving photo closer): Now you are closer to it than I am.

Benton: I would hesitate to pass opinion on it. I am afraid the artist wouldn't like it.[129]

Benton's confusion was gleefully reported by the press, especially *Newsweek*, which featured Crawford's painting – on its side – in an article on the hearings and subsequently in its Letters to the Editor section, where one subscriber humorously identified the painting as a portrait of Frank Sinatra with a microphone.[130]

Such rampant hostility did little to ease Crawford's postwar reentry into the art world. Upon his discharge in 1945 he had felt adrift; he likened being "sprung" from the Army to leaving Leavenworth, but a Leavenworth in which he had learned to live. His putative liberation was followed by what he described as a one-and-a-half-year-long hysteria during which he attempted to regain his bearings.[131] Psychologically unprepared to resume painting, he had extended his job with the weather service. His Bikini assignment had been but one of many efforts to create a niche for himself, including an attempt to prepare a book on his India photos and weather maps as well as to enhance his skills in the applied arts through enrollment in Moholy-Nagy's Institute of Design, Chicago.[132] While Crawford recognized the impossibility of returning to the art he had been producing in 1942, he nevertheless wanted to reclaim many of the values and ideas that had gone into "storage" during the war.[133] He accepted the offer of a summer teaching job in Hawaii in 1947, hoping it would give him the time to himself he desperately needed to "pull together some post war threads that were really ripped."[134]

Given Crawford's difficult reentry into postwar society, and his loss of confidence in the social and individual benefits of industrial technology, he began to question the basic purpose of his work for the first time. He never questioned that he could make pictures or, in fact, that he even had the choice, but he did confess to feeling lower about his work than ever before.[135] Typically, however, his reaction was to persevere. Despite his uncertainty about his art, he wrote to Peggy that he "never tried to do anything but make it better. Yes I know the payoff is the real McCoy if one does that. . . . If the boys sometimes don't like the work, they respect it because . . . I have told them the truth as I have found it. O.K. let's paint some more pictures trying to know the right paths and keeping on them."[136]

For Crawford these right paths entailed the restraint and ordering of emotions. As formulated on his trip to India, he believed that art was essentially constructive – that it was the antithesis of chaos. By 1949 he was openly identifying his goal as "finding and expressing . . . a bit of order."[137] He still held that his non-rational faculties supplied the impetus for his work, but henceforth this emotional component would be thoroughly contained by his desire for a satisfying pictorial logic, a desire that would push him further toward abstraction. No longer would making an "interpretative" comment on the external world compel him. Indeed, rather than insist on an emotional relationship with his subject, Crawford pronounced it "possible to say something pictorially interesting about anything."[138] This commitment to the primacy of formal values over subjective communication would make Crawford's postwar pictorial world a rather hermetic one. Because he operated primarily in the realm of formal order and beauty and forfeited easily recognized images, his paintings became far less publicly accessible than his Precisionist works had been. The overt emotional reticence of these postwar works corresponded to Crawford's deeply restrained temperament. Even to his friends he revealed little about himself. That Crawford possessed an almost spiritual side is clear; that he seldom allowed its expression is equally clear. Indeed, his very appropriation of abstraction might have been, as Lloyd Goodrich has suggested about others, a means of circumventing painful emotional realities through the creation of a world in which he had full control.[139]

Behind Crawford's obsession with control and order was an intense discipline. "There has always got to be on the part of any serious painter a well disciplined approach to his life," he wrote.[140] Having committed himself to art, he let nothing come between himself and his painting. He realized that to accomplish anything of significance long hours of hard work and a willingness to persist even when discouraged were essential. Not to perform to the utmost of his ability seemed to go against a moral law and made him feel he had broken trust with himself. Believing that an artist must vigilantly keep in training for work, Crawford attempted to organize his life to make it as conducive to artistic growth as possible.[141] This regimen ideally involved long, undisturbed periods of quiet and an avoidance of fatigue and the deadening of imagination that attended contact with trivial or superficial society. He even tried to limit his companions to those he felt would abet good painting by offering emotional and intellectual stimulation or by providing practical business contacts. For others, he announced to Peggy, "I shall have less and less time. . . ."[142]

Crawford's work ethic extended well beyond aesthetics. If he became interested in a subject, he pursued it with the same unassailable discipline and focus he brought to his painting. Though soft-spoken and reticent in public, Crawford's practice of total commitment accounted for the undeniable charisma others perceived in him. Nor was he unappreciative of such commitment in others: after watching a swimming meet in 1947, he wrote to Peggy that the swimmers were "close to artists. They are in there to do the thing as well as it is humanly possible.

There are no compromises. Maybe they could make it 'prettier' for the public, but they don't."[143] A similar appreciation would draw him to bull and cock fights, car races, New Orleans jazz, and the religious parades in Seville, Spain. He felt every sport presented possibilities for plastic beauty and that the physical challenges they entailed were analogous to the challenge of the blank canvas. Both arenas required control, audacity, tension, and skill. He likened the remark made by the race-car driver Sterling Moss about the driver's commitment to the curve to his own commitment in painting. The "strange mélange of madness and exquisite precision" which he identified at Le Mans was precisely the quality he sought in his own work.[144]

Despite Crawford's misgivings about the direction of his postwar work, his pictorial output remained relatively high. Yet only in 1949 did he feel he had fully passed through the aesthetic doldrums of the preceding years. Reflecting on the earlier, Precisionist stage of his career, he had written in 1946 that "it seems to me that a young painter or student uses (frequently well) the ideals of others. As he grows a bit, he is more dependent upon his own. Then the going gets rather

69. *Factory with Yellow Center Shape*, 1947. Oil on canvas, 28 x 40 inches (71.1 x 101.6 cm). Ralston Crawford Estate, New York.

lonely."[145] He paraphrased Degas' observation that a twenty-one-year-old with talent was easy to find, a talented forty-five-year-old harder. By the end of the decade he felt he had found his own aesthetic voice. Acknowledging that the "1st 20 years in this field are certainly the easiest," he confided that he was now "on his own."[146] By the spring of 1949 he could write that "I am making the dream and will presently find a place to go with it."[147]

70. *Boxcars, Minneapolis*, 1949–52. Oil on canvas, 30 x 42 inches (76.2 x 106.7 cm). Ralston Crawford Estate, New York.

The paintings which manifested Crawford's newly found aesthetic voice were no longer exclusively limited to a single visual image or idea, but were as easily derived from experiences of disparate times and places (Figs. 69–72). "My paintings vary in degree of directness to things seen. Some are synthetic expressions of many visual experiences, others constitute a distorted but accentuated vision of quite simple forms."[148] In the first category were dense and complex paintings such as *Third Avenue Elevated* (Fig 73), Crawford's amalgamation of the lush color of Hawaii with the patterns of light and shadow on the Third Avenue Elevated (Figs. 74, 75). In the second category, "accentuated visions," Crawford offered quite direct translations. Yet even here, the paintings' constituent shapes often appeared totally abstract and autonomous because Crawford radically cropped his source motif. Nor did he feel any obligation to reveal it pictorially:

71. *Fisherman's Wharf, San Francisco*, 1947–50. Oil on canvas, 30 x 40 inches (76.2 x 101.6 cm). Private collection.

72. *Boxcar, Minneapolis #2*, 1949–61. Oil on canvas, 60 x 40 inches (152.4 x 101.6 cm). Ralston Crawford Estate, New York.

73. *Third Avenue Elevated,* 1949. Oil on canvas, 29¾ x 40⅛ inches (75.6 x 101.9 cm). Walker Art Center, Minneapolis; Gift of the Gilbert M. Walker Fund.

"the forms . . . may be absent to the viewer of the work, or even to myself. . . ."[149] Once he had started painting, the formal requirements took over and the original stimuli became unimportant. In this way he ensured that his paintings were independent objects, "related to but having an existence entirely apart from the subject."[150]

The same principles that applied to form held true for color, which was likewise either synthetic or an intensification of a single experience. Color ceased being a descriptive tool and became a means of establishing shape. The vibrant palette and elimination of modeling and softly modulated color tones he had introduced in his Bikini pictures remained his vehicles of expression. Uninflected color areas divided by crisp demarcations would henceforth characterize his work.

As Crawford's interest shifted from the single-image impact of his Precisionist works to dynamic color-form relationships, pictorial tension became for him painting's most durable and engaging component. To maintain interest in pictorial structure, he juxtaposed contrasting types of forms and colors, likening such oppositions to "pictorial counterpoint — the juxtaposing of one melody or theme in relation to another, or to several."[151] This analogy between music and painting was one he pursued throughout his life: in a notebook entry on Leonardo da Vinci's *Virgin of the Rocks*, he marveled at the painting's "wealth of contrapuntal activity" and on the "cross melodic references" produced by blues in different parts of the canvas.[152] In his own work, he established a dynamic, contradictory spatial network by having shapes advance and recede simultaneously. In *Third Avenue Elevated* (Fig. 73), for example, movement does not proceed *into* space from a single-point perspective as it did with his Precisionist paintings, but instead moves rhythmically across the canvas surface by means of

74. *Third Avenue Elevated, Horizontal,* 1948. Silver gelatin print, 6½ x 9½ inches (16.5 x 24.1 cm). Ralston Crawford Estate, New York.

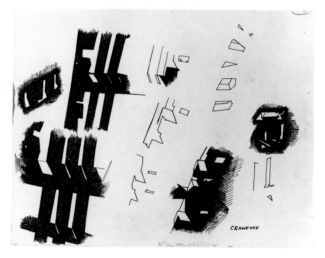

75. *Untitled (Third Avenue Elevated Tracks),* c. 1949. Pen and ink on paper, 11 x 13¾ inches (27.9 x 34.9 cm). Ralston Crawford Estate, New York.

oblique and angular shapes which twist and curve at different "melodic" tempos.

What particularly distinguished Crawford's paintings of the late 1940s from earlier ones was his reliance on photography as a springboard for image-making. In 1942, before joining the service, he had produced a series of photographs on architectural subjects (Figs. 79–81). He resumed photography during his 1945 trip to India (Fig. 82). By 1948, Crawford's photographs had begun to receive scattered critical attention.[153] Although he had used photographs as early as the thirties as source material for his paintings, it was not until the end of the 1940s that the medium began to have a definitive impact on his oils. Describing his efforts in painting during the 1949-50 school term, he wrote that he had "learned how to press my luck . . . to recognize any little vein of ore . . . and to dig out of it all that I can."[154] This "little vein of ore" was photography, a medium he credited with contributing to the "making [of] better pictures in oil."[155] Indeed, a com-

76. *Untitled (Wharf Objects)*, c. 1948. Silver gelatin print, 3¼ x 5⅛ inches (8.3 x 13 cm). Ralston Crawford Estate, New York.

parison between his paintings, drawings, and photographic images (Figs. 76–78, 83–85, 87–89) reveals how photography allowed him to retain his connection to the original source motif while simultaneously creating abstract and pictorially complex compositions.

The results of Crawford's postwar pictorial activities were presented in January 1950 at what would be his last exhibition with the Downtown Gallery. Although he had fully succeeded in creating a subjective geometric idiom, he had charted an unpopular course, one that violated both the conservatives' attachment to a recognizable image and the vanguard rage for a Surrealist-derived, painterly art. As a consequence, his exhibition was not so much derided as ig-

77. *Wharf Objects, Santa Barbara*, 1948. Oil on canvas, 26 x 36 inches (66 x 91.4 cm). Collection of Paul J. Leaman, Jr.

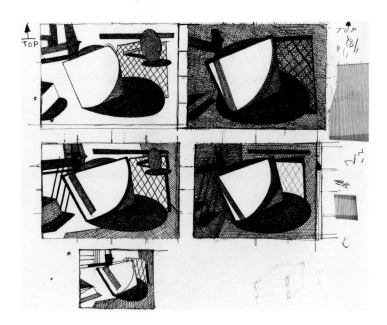

78. *Untitled (Wharf Objects)*, c. 1948. Pen and ink on paper, 11¼ x 11⅝ inches (28.6 x 29.5 cm). Ralston Crawford Estate, New York.

80. *Grain Elevators, Buffalo*, 1942. Silver gelatin print, 9 x 8⅜ inches (22.9 x 21.3 cm). Ralston Crawford Estate, New York.

79. *Grain Elevators, Buffalo*, 1942. Silver gelatin print, 13½ x 8⅞ inches (34.3 x 22.5 cm). Ralston Crawford Estate, New York.

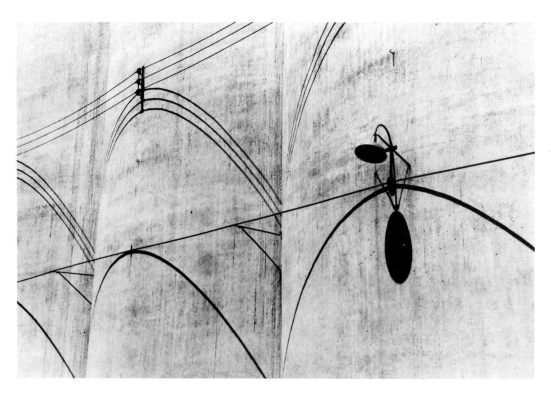

81. *Untitled (Shadows on Grain Elevators, Buffalo)*, c. 1942. Silver gelatin print, 6¼ x 9½ inches (15.9 x 24.1 cm). Ralston Crawford Estate, New York.

nored: only two tepid notices appeared in the press. For Halpert, Crawford's work was simply too abstract. Her dissatisfaction had originated much earlier, at the time Crawford first started to move from a realistic to a more advanced visual style. Crawford, for his part, had become annoyed by 1945 with her pronouncements that Davis was the "best abstractionist" in the gallery; throughout the war he had cautioned Peggy about too much social interaction with Halpert.[156] By 1947 relations had deteriorated to such an extent that Crawford sensed there was a good chance of severing ties with Halpert – "the ice is very thin now and I'd like to do the breaking."[157] A year later Halpert had stopped promoting him with anything near the enthusiasm she marshaled for her other artists, with the result that the first half of 1948 produced only $512 worth of sales, minus her one-third commission. The failure of Crawford's 1950 exhibition confirmed her misgivings that he was too abstract for her gallery. Three years later – having given him no subsequent shows – she attempted (unsuccessfully) to pass him over to Charles Alan, who was opening new exhibition premises and had agreed to take some of her artists.

Crawford fared no better in vanguard circles, given the Abstract Expressionist wave that had swept New York by 1950. Abstract Expressionism was antithetical

82. *Untitled (The Burning Ghats #2)*, 1945. Silver gelatin print, 10⅛ x 13¼ inches (25.7 x 33.7 cm). Ralston Crawford Estate, New York.

to virtually everything Crawford and his work represented.[158] Stylistically, Abstract Expressionism strove to avoid all reference to the Synthetic Cubist concepts that characterized Crawford's geometric abstractionism; thematically, it favored mythic and totemic imagery and the depiction of the artist's emotional state. In the interests of establishing a uniquely American cultural expression, Abstract Expressionism replaced French "taste" and "finish" with what was regarded as specifically American: force, crudeness, and virility. And, finally, its view of the artist as virile and bohemian was diametrically opposed to Crawford's urbane posture and nattily dressed look.

83. *On the Sundeck*, 1948. Oil on canvas, 30 x 45 inches (76.2 x 114.3 cm). Ralston Crawford Estate, New York.

That Crawford viewed painting as an act of discovery in which partially evolved conceptions were extended and clarified did link him with the Abstract Expressionists, but only tangentially, since his "discoveries" were generally limited to premeditated manipulations.[159] His deep-seated animosity toward subjective displays and his elimination of all evidence of the picture-making process made his work seem to lack the animating human spirit. And his subject matter, far from being mythic, still highlighted the industrial scene which had, at best, lost its prestige and, at worst, been discredited. Moreover, in the context of Abstract Expressionism's emphatic rejection of French models, Crawford's lifelong attraction to European art and European culture was considered retrogressive. The chasm was dramatically revealed in a symposium on the French avant-garde

84. *Untitled (On the Sundeck)*, c. 1947. Pen and ink on paper, 10⅝ x 13⅞ inches (27 x 35.2 cm). Ralston Crawford Estate, New York.

85. *Shadows on Boat Deck*, 1947. Silver gelatin print, 8⅝ x 12½ inches (21.9 x 31.8 cm). Ralston Crawford Estate, New York.

conducted in 1953 by *The Art Digest* in which the critic Clement Greenberg repudiated the tameness and suavity of French forms while Crawford, as if oblivious to the battle for aesthetic supremacy, claimed that contemporary French art was still a vital force.[160] He also spoke of the esteem with which artists were held in France irrespective of external signs of success. Crawford's statement underscored his long-standing affection for France, which he began visiting regularly after 1950.

Crawford was not alone in finding his work supplanted by Abstract Expressionism. By 1948 the geometric abstractionists who had previously stood for what

86. *Mackinaw—Oden*, c. 1946. Silver gelatin print, 5¾ x 8½ inches (14.6 x 21.6 cm). Ralston Crawford Estate, New York.

was most advanced in American art had been swept aside because their work was perceived as being too closely linked to the School of Paris. This was the fate suffered by Byron Browne. When Samuel Kootz opened his gallery in 1949, he eliminated Browne from his favored circle and rather unceremoniously dumped his work at Gimbels to be sold in bulk at cut-rate prices, thus thoroughly depressing Browne's market – a rejection from which Browne never fully recovered.[161] Precisionists such as Sheeler had a slightly easier time with the new realignments, for even though they fell out of favor, their reputations as "established masters" were not as affected by the power shuffle. Unfortunately, though Crawford had earlier been identified with the Precisionist movement, he was too young, and his association with it too short-lived, to be accorded similar protection.

Crawford's exclusion from the art community after 1950 became endemic. Compounding his aesthetic disjunction was his self-imposed physical insulation. He ceased to associate with artistic contemporaries and began to draw his friends from other fields. In order to ensure a minimal financial security for his family, he accepted jobs throughout the 1950s as a visiting instructor at colleges and universities. That these assignments often took him out of New York only aggravated his loss of aesthetic visibility.[162] His shows during the last twenty-eight years of his life were reviewed only perfunctorily; since he rarely appeared at art functions, the presumption by at least one artist was that he had died soon after the war.[163]

Yet, although he railed against the mediocre denizens of most of the art departments with which he had to contend, and lamented that teaching was not to be confused with a good life,[164] these semester-long stretches away from New York could have allowed him respite from a world in which he had been relegated to the past. And while teaching interfered with his work, it also threw him into company with individuals who supported his vision of himself as a major artist. A corresponding smugness about his own self-importance permeated the lecture tours he made in 1950 and 1956: the hint of pomposity which precipitated these speaking engagements to relatively uninformed groups from junior and technical high schools and public service organizations around the Midwest suggests a somewhat distorted and uncritical appraisal of his own aesthetic position.

But it also spoke affirmatively for the unswerving faith he maintained in the quality of his work during the last quarter-century of his life, despite the paucity of external validation. Indeed, his conviction, derived initially from Breckenridge, that the act of painting far exceeded the importance of sales or press notices became more pronounced. Seemingly undaunted by the failure of his 1950 exhibition, he wrote to Peggy that the audience "can't be expected in these 20 minute tours to follow 4 years of thought."[165] Crawford probably could have salvaged a certain level of critical and financial success if he had been willing to recycle earlier Precisionist images. But, as he later wrote, "I am not interested, and never have been, in 'playing it safe.'"[166] Believing it was fatal to the artist's spirit to stop evolving, he adamantly refused to repeat himself; he preferred pictorially unfamiliar territory even to the extent of being "[un]afraid to paint a bad picture."[167] Moreover, he dismissed the public's demand for a single, identifiable mode as having more to do with marketing strategies than with art, and vilified "trademark" art as formulaic.[168] Unlike most of his contemporaries, he had no investment in conspicuous individuality or aesthetic novelty and counseled his students to worry not about being avant-garde, but rather about being themselves. "In connection with looking at pictures and painting them, the point is to forget one's originality or rather one's concern with it. . . . I . . . look to other expressions with the hope that I shall be moved and indebted. The cult of the individual has reached absurd proportions in some parts of the art world."[169]

87. *Freight Cars, Minneapolis*, 1949. Oil on canvas, 40 x 30 inches (101.6 x 76.2 cm). Collection of Wesley Love.

Photography took on an added importance in Crawford's work after 1950 – precisely the moment when critical response to his paintings was ebbing. His subject matter involved two primary themes: one dealing with abstract, architectural images and another focused on New Orleans jazz musicians and their milieu. Both architectural and genre subjects had been part of Crawford's repertoire in the 1940s (Figs. 79–81, 86), but they did not occupy his exclusive attention until after 1950 (Fig. 90).

Crawford's jazz series began in 1949, when he joined several of his students from Louisiana State University at Baton Rouge for a weekend outing to New Orleans to listen to jazz. In retrospect, his immediate infatuation with the music and its performers might have been predicted: as early as 1938 he had notified the Guggenheim Foundation of his desire to paint southern black life (see p. 45), and during the late 1930s and 1940s he and Peggy had passed long hours with Stuart and Roselle Davis listening to jazz recordings. Crawford spent many of the weekends remaining of the 1949-50 school term in New Orleans, coming to love the French Quarter of the city whose slow pace, civilized manners, and neighborhood quality made him feel far more at home than he did in New York. Over the next twenty-eight years, he would return frequently to listen to the city's music and photographically chronicle its world – its buildings, jazz men, singers, nightclubs, and street parades (Figs. 91–97). Here was a "deeply humanizing"[170] world

 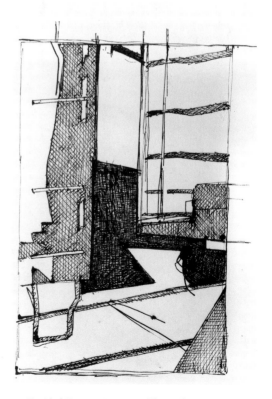

88. *Untitled (Boxcars)*, c. 1949. Pen and ink on paper, 10⅛ x 6⅝ inches (25.7 x 16.8 cm). Ralston Crawford Estate, New York.

89. *Untitled (Boxcars)*, c. 1949. Silver gelatin print, 9½ x 6⅜ inches (24.1 x 16.2 cm). Ralston Crawford Estate, New York.

90. *Ambulatory Splint Company*, 1954. Silver gelatin print, 8¼ x 12¼ inches (21 x 31.1 cm). Ralston Crawford Estate, New York.

91. *Dancer at 500 Club*, 1950s. Silver gelatin print, 9½ x 7¹¹⁄₁₆ inches (24.1 x 19.5 cm). Ralston Crawford Estate, New York.

without pretense or artifice that provided nourishment for his work and released in him a wellspring of feelings for which he was less able to find expression elsewhere. Yet even within this environment, Crawford remained essentially an outsider. He was trusted and liked by the musicians, whom he numbered among his best friends. But he never attempted to eradicate the barrier that race and social position created; the musicians, though they occasionally visited his home, always referred to him as Mr. Crawford.

Crawford's photographs of New Orleans, taken between 1950 and the mid-1970s, provide a comprehensive portrait of the city's musical life, an achieve-

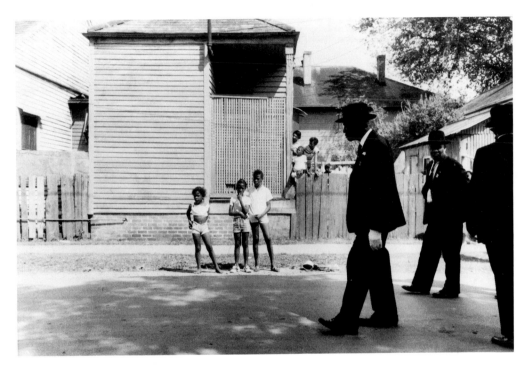

92. *Young Men's Olympian Benevolent Association*, 1958. Silver gelatin print, 6¼ x 9⁹⁄₁₆ inches (15.9 x 24.3 cm). Ralston Crawford Estate, New York.

ment he noted in his application to the Guggenheim Foundation in 1953. By that time he had assembled over 6500 negatives; when he died in 1978 he had amassed close to 10,000 finished prints. That Crawford took on the task of documenting New Orleans life bears witness to his inherently methodical instincts. His commitment to thoroughness permeated the series, with the result that some of his favorite photographs do not totally transcend the parochial interest of subject matter and are more important as documents than as autonomous images. To this documentary focus was added his understandable desire for financial remuneration, which explains his attempt in 1950 to interest *Fortune* in commissioning a portfolio of photographs surveying blacks in the South.[171] That having failed, he next proposed to produce a book on jazz in collaboration with his friend the jazz scholar Richard Allen. Because Allen did not submit the whole text quickly enough the book never materialized. But through Allen, Crawford was named a

93. *Advertising the Dance, New Orleans,* 1953. Silver gelatin print, 9½ x 13½ inches (24.1 x 34.3 cm). Ralston Crawford Estate, New York.

94. *Beauty Queens with Wine Glasses,* 1952. Silver gelatin print, 6½ x 9½ inches (16.5 x 24.1 cm). Ralston Crawford Estate, New York.

95. *John T. Lala, Proprietor, "Big 25,"* 1950s. Silver gelatin print, 13½ x 10¾ inches (34.3 x 27.3 cm). Ralston Crawford Estate, New York.

97. *Dancer at the Dew Drop Inn,* c. 1950. Silver gelatin print, 9½ x 7½ inches (24.1 x 19.1 cm). Ralston Crawford Estate, New York.

96. *George Lewis, New Orleans,* 1950. Silver gelatin print, 9⁹/₁₆ x 7¹¹/₁₆ inches (24.3 x 19.5 cm). Ralston Crawford Estate, New York.

photography consultant to the newly established Archive of Jazz at Tulane University. By 1961, over 800 of Crawford's prints had been purchased by the Archive.

Crawford's New Orleans photographs are unique within his oeuvre not only for their human subject matter but for their lack of premeditation. In order to capture the spontaneity and ebullient spirit of his subjects, Crawford necessarily forfeited control and precision. He compensated by taking endless exposures of single events, which he described as "no more [significant] in relation to the final photograph than a few pencil lines would mean to a completed oil painting."[172] He worked in series in his paintings as well, but the serial character of his photography underscored his view that no single shot was final;[173] that the truth was not absolute but was only partially revealed at every instant. In painting, by contrast, one had time in which to incorporate a plurality of observations within a single composition.

98. *Coulee Dam Staging Area #2*, 1972. Silver gelatin print, 9 x 13½ inches (22.9 x 34.3 cm). Ralston Crawford Estate, New York.

99. *Untitled (Ring and Shadow on Wall)*, 1969. Silver gelatin print, 13⁷⁄₁₆ x 9¹⁄₁₆ inches (34.1 x 23 cm). Ralston Crawford Estate, New York.

100. *St. Louis Cemetery, New Orleans,* 1950s. Silver gelatin print, 9½ x 6⁷⁄₁₆ inches (24.1 x 16.4 cm). Ralston Crawford Estate, New York.

101. *Untitled (New Orleans Still Life),* c. 1951. Silver gelatin print, 2½ x 3⁹⁄₁₆ inches (6.4 x 9 cm). Ralston Crawford Estate, New York.

Crawford's second category of photographs – architectural or industrial subjects – relied for their success on the same Synthetic Cubist vocabulary that informed his oils (Figs. 98, 99). Their essentially abstract approach is particularly evident in the series of "still lifes" of New Orleans cemeteries he began in the 1950s (Figs. 100, 101). Attracted by the intense white light which bathed these plaster graves, Crawford created works of fine-tuned abstract integrity in which space was compressed into planes and deployed into patterns. Despite the potential poignancy of the site – the humid climate of New Orleans accelerated the deterioration of the graves – his primary interest lay with the formal properties of the structures and their textural juxtapositions of smooth plaster against crumbling bricks and peeling paint.

Crawford never doubted that his photographs were valid aesthetic statements. They nonetheless occupied a less exalted realm than did his painting, owing mostly to the necessity of having to "collaborate" with an unalterable, preexisting subject. Unlike other art forms, the photographer could not modify configuration or color without violating the inherent truthfulness of the medium. In an informal discussion with students at Tulane University Crawford discussed the relative merits of photography and painting. No photograph, he declared, could compare in quality to the "Catalonian frescoes" or move into the first rank of art.[174]

Crawford's photographs and paintings were mutually interdependent. His photographs, he frequently acknowledged, "followed his paintings" – as, for example, in his 1951 shots of the bombed-out buildings in Cologne, which he called photographs of his Bikini pictures (Fig. 114). However, in considering his photographs as "paintings already completed,"[175] Crawford did not mean that he returned to the exact sites of earlier paintings to photograph them; rather, he was drawn to subjects which reminded him of those he had already explored in oil. "One loves the shapes that he sees clearly – in varied continuities," he wrote.[176] Photography was thus not so much a means of discovering something unknown as it was a clarifier of observations and thoughts already revealed.

But Crawford's photographs were not always a step behind his oils. He habitually carried a camera, so that photography often functioned as a journal or sketch pad, providing inspiration and information for future paintings. Yet even those paintings which most closely followed his photographs were rarely direct transcriptions. In his paintings, he often highlighted aspects that seemed visually auxiliary in the photograph while simultaneously simplifying or eliminating photographic details that contributed to the recognizability of the site. One feature he especially exploited was the form-making capabilities of light and shadow. "Light," as Sheeler had said, "is the great designer."[177] It could obliterate the divisions between forms or create new and seemingly arbitrary ones by means of shadow. Light had been a component of Crawford's work as early as the 1930s when he had used it to bathe architectural forms in an ambient intensity. By the fifties, his work manifested the Impressionists' implicit assertion that painting was about light – a quality he, too, claimed to be depicting. But unlike the Impressionists, who analyzed and broke light up into its color components, Crawford appreciated the image potential of shadows. He had introduced shadows into his painting soon after purchasing his first camera in 1938, but, as in *Maitland Bridge #2* (Fig. 46), he rendered them realistically – as shadows. As he became more steeped in photography, he began to treat them as autonomous and fully saturated forms on a par with solids. In *New Orleans Still Life* (Fig. 102), for example, the blue and black triangular form to the left of the ochre vase is just such a shadow.

This treatment of the evanescent and the solid as equally commanding pictorial elements increased the abstract quotient of Crawford's compositions. In pictures such as *Fishing Boats #6*, Crawford further manipulated visual sources as it suited his compositional needs (Figs. 103, 104). Here, negative spaces are rendered as solids, areas of light and shadow are reversed, and visually insignificant divisions within forms are painted different colors, while negative spaces and their contingent masses are joined into single color areas. Yet however abstract the results, Crawford's paintings remain linked to concrete sources. As had been true earlier, a comparison between his photographs and paintings of the 1950s – including *New Orleans Still Life* and *Fishing Boats #6* (Figs. 102, 104) – bears witness to his claim that he "never painted anything he didn't see."[178] With

102. *New Orleans Still Life*, 1951. Oil on canvas, 30 x 45 inches (76.2 x 114.3 cm). Ralston Crawford Estate, New York.

104. *Fishing Boats #6*, 1956. Oil on canvas, 40 x 30 inches (101.6 x 76.2 cm). Ralston Crawford Estate, New York.

103. *Star of the Occident, Croix de Vie, Vendée, France,* 1955. Silver gelatin print, 9⅞ x 6⅝ inches (25.1 x 16.8 cm). Ralston Crawford Estate, New York.

105. *New Orleans #8*, 1957–58. Oil on canvas, 28¾ x 21¼ inches (73 x 54 cm). Ralston Crawford Estate, New York.

Crawford, the visual took precedence over the conceptual, which may help explain why there is always a freshness and individuality in his paintings. Clearly Crawford's genius lay in his acute powers of perception rather than those of arbitrary invention.

Though occasionally Crawford's subject matter was based on earlier drawings and photographs, it generally mirrored his more recent experiences, including his trips to New Orleans (Figs. 105–108); compositions derived from an automobile graveyard he saw on a teaching assignment in Boulder, Colorado, in 1958; or his Construction series, also of 1958, inspired by a commission he and nine

106. *New Orleans #7*, 1954–56. Oil on canvas, 40 x 28 inches (101.6 x 71.1 cm). The Lane Collection.

107. *New Orleans #5*, 1954. Oil on canvas, 50 x 36 inches (127 x 91.4 cm). Sheldon Memorial Art Gallery, University of Nebraska—Lincoln; F.M. Hall Collection.

other painters received from the Wolfson Construction Company to interpret the skyscraper being erected at 100 Church Street in Manhattan (Figs. 109, 110). In alternating shapes set obliquely into space with those placed parallel to the picture plane, Crawford created a highly original and dynamic sense of space. This same focus – on the relationship between the flatness of the picture plane and the illusion of three dimensions – had occupied him as a beginning painter.

From the 1950s on, Crawford's work alternated between the complex, multifaceted vocabulary which had entered his work during the war and a more reductive expression. *Port Clyde #1* (Fig. 111), from the latter group, was composed of large, simple shapes, stripped of all decorative accessories. Its stark abstraction and pictorial tension stand as a monument to the exquisite equilibrium and tautness with which Crawford constructed his pictures. In contrast, the jagged forms of *First Avenue #1* (Fig. 112), which float ominously across a flat,

108. *New Orleans #9*, 1957–58. Oil on canvas, 19¾ x 28¾ inches (50.2 x 73 cm). Ralston Crawford Estate, New York.

rectangular space as if fronting a stage set, drew their associations from the destruction Crawford had witnessed in Bikini and Cologne. Crawford had made a brief excursion from Paris to Cologne in 1951 to purchase a camera. Once there, he became mesmerized by the rubble and bombed-out buildings which littered the city and reminded him of the effects of the bomb and its capacity for destruction. For Crawford, Bikini and Cologne were equivalent. Not surprisingly, given his sentiment that "Bikini is not easy to forget,"[179] Crawford returned to the theme of destruction throughout his life.

109. *Construction #5*, 1958. Oil on canvas, 36 x 26 inches (91.4 x 66 cm). Ralston Crawford Estate, New York.

110. *Construction #7*, 1958. Oil on canvas, 24 x 18 inches (61 x 45.7 cm). Collection of Mr. and Mrs. Richard B. Freeman.

111. *Port Clyde #1*, c. 1965. Oil on canvas, 30¼ x 40¼ inches (76.8 x 102.2 cm). Collection of Mr. and Mrs. Graham Stafford.

Yet Crawford's essentially constructive view of the world prevailed. (It accounted, in fact, for his ability to appreciate the aesthetics and emotionally charged aspects of bull and cock fighting and Grand Prix races without capitulating to their destructive potential.) Even during the war Crawford had affirmed that "it is difficult . . . but very important, to remember the many aspects of reality to-day. . . . We must hold to our beliefs in the constructive, the positive vital drives that concern mankind in various periods."[180] He had concomitantly cautioned Peggy not to be unnerved by the current "historical sequences" and stressed that those with positive viewpoints must assert themselves.[181] With respect to Cologne, he had been both "sick *and* delighted" – sickened by what he saw, but conscious that he had to be delighted if he were to make art out of his experiences.[182] "I could not make it brutal," he later wrote. "I wanted people to look at it as a statement they could look at again without getting ill, but never forgetting what went on there."[183] Likewise in 1958, when recollections of Bikini and the plane wrecks of World War II were summoned forth by the large assembly of demolished automobiles he saw in Colorado (Fig. 113), his reaction was one of pleasure – "the positive nature of seeing transcended the dreary connotations of these shapes."[184]

112. *First Avenue #1*, 1953–54. Oil on canvas, 32 x 40 inches (81.3 x 101.6 cm). Ralston Crawford Estate, New York.

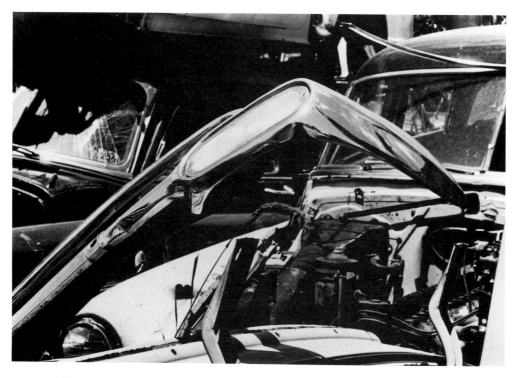

113. *Untitled (Junk Cars)*, 1958. Silver gelatin print, 6½ x 9½ inches (16.5 x 24.1 cm). Ralston Crawford Estate, New York.

The 1950s also mark Crawford's intense involvement with lithography. After his first experiments with the medium in 1940 and 1941, he did not produce any prints until 1949, when he represented his memories of Bikini in *Crack-Up* and *Crack-Up Fragments*. Although ostensibly of Bikini, these lithographs drew their inspiration from the war in general and, specifically, from drawings he had made during his service with the weather division.[185] Encouraged by the outcome of his lithographic experiments, Crawford arranged to travel to Paris in 1951-52 to work in the lithography shops of Edmund Desjobert and Mourlot Fréres. The first prints he executed there were based on photographs he had taken of bombed-out Cologne buildings (Figs. 114, 115). As he described them, these fourteen lithographs "put down some of the feelings and thoughts . . . about the cracked-up, rotten, manure-heap facets of this society and the good and noble aspects of human existence *now* and in *all* societies."[186]

Given Crawford's earlier comparison of the visual effects of Bikini – and, by extension, Cologne – with the smashing of a tin can by an elevated train,[187] it was perhaps fitting that he produced eight lithographs of the Third Avenue Elevated on this same trip to Paris. Already in 1948 Crawford had taken endless photographs of the various patterns of light on the el and had subsequently translated a number of them into drawings and paintings (Figs. 73–75). Now, in 1951, the image underwent another metamorphosis, becoming more stark and reductive

114. *Cologne,* 1951. Silver gelatin print, 9 x 13⁷⁄₁₆ inches (22.9 x 34.1 cm). Ralston Crawford Estate, New York.

115. *Cologne Landscape #6,* 1951. Color lithograph, 14⁷⁄₈ x 21¹⁄₈ inches (37.8 x 53.7 cm). Whitney Museum of American Art, New York; Gift of Charles Simon   71.77.

than in either previous incarnation (Fig. 116). The simplified geometry and rhythmical balance between light and dark in these and, indeed, all of Crawford's works can be seen as anticipating the hard-edged and geometric painting style that came into vogue in the 1960s. In this regard, Crawford's work is particularly aligned to that of Ellsworth Kelly, whose paintings of the 1950s likewise relied on the form-making potential of shadow (Fig. 117).

Crawford returned to Paris for lithography sessions on three occasions over the next eight years – in 1954-55, 1957, and 1959. He described these sessions as providing nourishment for his paintings and as having "an emancipatory effect on my entire function as an artist."[188] The predominantly black-and-white palette of these lithographs and their simplified graphic style underscored his contention that lithography "is a most reductive medium."[189] During the 1950s, in Paris and America, Crawford frequently recast in lithographs the Cologne theme as well as that of New Orleans cemeteries, Minneapolis freight yards, French fishing wharves, and Spanish bullfights (Figs. 118, 119). As in *Third Avenue Elevated #4* and *L'Étoile de l'Occident* (Figs. 121, 123), these lithographs often echoed images from his drawings, paintings, and photographs (Figs. 120, 122).

During the last twenty-five years of his life, when painting sales and exhibitions were relatively minimal, Crawford's lithographs had a lively market among print collectors. Even at the time of his death, the majority of his works in public collections were lithographs. Unfortunately, Crawford's relative success with print enthusiasts had virtually no effect on his standing in the art world, for print collectors formed a specialized audience with little influence on, or contact with, art's larger arena.

116. *Third Avenue Elevated #1*, 1951. Color lithograph, 10⅜ x 17¹⁵⁄₁₆ inches (26.4 x 45.6 cm). Whitney Museum of American Art, New York; Gift of Charles Simon   71.144.

117. Ellsworth Kelly, *La Combe, I,* 1950. Oil on canvas, 38¼ x 63¾ inches (97.2 x 161.9 cm). Collection of the artist.

118. *New Orleans #4A,* 1953. Lithograph, 19½ x 13 inches (49.5 x 33 cm). Whitney Museum of American Art, New York; Gift of Charles Simon 71.122.

119. *Toro Heads*, 1957. Lithograph, 19¾ x 26 inches (50.2 x 66 cm). Whitney Museum of American Art, New York; Gift of Charles Simon   71.148.

Apart from print exhibitions and the occasional reproduction of his photographs in jazz publications, Crawford's primary interaction with the art world during the 1950s was occasioned by his exhibitions at the Grace Borgenicht Gallery, which represented him after Halpert.[190] As had become the pattern, reviews were few. Only three of Crawford's paintings were reproduced in national magazines during the entire decade, and one of them was on its side.[191]

The decade of the 1960s began more propitiously. The Walker Art Center's "The Precisionist View in American Art," the first comprehensive museum exhibition to survey this movement, opened in 1961. The show featured Crawford's work prominently, alongside that of classic American figures such as Sheeler, Demuth, and O'Keeffe. Given the show's arrival on the eve of Pop Art, with its relatively hard-edge style, one would have expected an end to the critical ennui which had settled over many of these artists' reputations during the heyday of Abstract Expressionism. Unfortunately, the show was slightly too early: it closed a few months before Pop Art captured the attention of the art world. As a result, Precisionism was seen strictly as a historical phenomenon lacking any contemporary reverberations. At least one critic, still in the clutches of Abstract Expressionism, viewed the work as "bloodless, thin, chilling."[192] For Crawford, the show had an especially adverse career effect, for it reinforced the view of him as an artist whose achievement lay in the past. Once again, he was exclusively

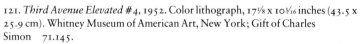

121. *Third Avenue Elevated #4*, 1952. Color lithograph, 17⅛ x 10³⁄₁₆ inches (43.5 x 25.9 cm). Whitney Museum of American Art, New York; Gift of Charles Simon   71.145.

120. *Third Avenue Elevated*, 1949. Silver gelatin print, 13⁷⁄₁₆ x 9¹⁄₁₆ inches (34.1 x 23 cm). Ralston Crawford Estate, New York.

122. *Fishing Boats #5*, 1956. Oil on canvas, 26¼ x 40 inches (66.7 x 101.6 cm). Private collection.

123. *L'Étoile de L'Occident,* 1955. Color lithograph, 10⅝ x 16¾ inches (27 x 42.5 cm). Whitney Museum of American Art, New York; Gift of Charles Simon   71.114.

identified as the creator of *Overseas Highway,* a presumption which his dealer at the time, Lee Nordness, was unable to challenge successfully.

Ignoring these winds of fashion, Crawford meanwhile preserved his characteristic optimism and continued to develop his work on his own terms. As he rhapsodized to Freeman: "The dream grows richer and deeper with each year, and with more substance."[193] By 1961 he had introduced into his vocabulary a linear element based on his observations of the fishing nets in the French seaside villages of Croix-de-Vie and St. Gilles, where he and his family summered in 1955, 1957 and 1962. Such linearity dramatically increased the complexity of his imagery. *Lobster Pots #3* (Fig. 124), with its highly charged and idiosyncratic palette of purples, blues, and light ochres, presents an assertive mosaic of patterned images. This effect, in combination with the larger canvas Crawford used here and in other paintings in the group, creates an impact both instantaneous and durable. The bold striations and graphic crosshatching of *St. Gilles #1* and *St. Gilles #4* (Figs. 125, 126) epitomized his goal of melding a variety of color shapes into unified wholes that would sustain repeated viewings. While the specific sources of this imagery remain visually inaccessible, these paintings nevertheless convey generalized impressions of the lobster pots and fishing tackle piled on the docks of these French seaside communities (Figs. 127, 128).

Summering in these villages anticipated a change in Crawford's life style during the 1960s. Apart from two visiting-artist assignments – in 1965 and 1966 – he ceased teaching during the last sixteen years of his life and spent his time traveling throughout the world. In addition to trips to New Orleans and Western Europe (Figs. 129–31), he went to North Africa, Tangier, the South Pacific, Indo-

124. *Lobster Pots #3*, 1960–63. Oil on canvas, 45 x 60 inches (114.3 x 152.4 cm). Ralston Crawford Estate, New York.

125. *St. Gilles #1*, 1962–63. Oil on canvas, 30 x 40 inches (76.2 x 101.6 cm). Ralston Crawford Estate, New York.

126. *St. Gilles #4*, 1962–63. Oil on canvas, 45 x 60 inches (114.3 x 152.4 cm). Ralston Crawford Estate, New York.

127. *Lobster Pots #2*, 1958. Oil on canvas, 30 x 40 inches (76.2 x 101.6 cm). Ralston Crawford Estate, New York.

128. *St. Croix*, 1957. Silver gelatin print, 11⅜ x 16½ inches (28.9 x 41.9 cm). Ralston Crawford Estate, New York.

nesia, Nepal, Egypt, Trinidad, and Guadalupe, among other places. Crawford could finance these excursions from sales of his work because Peggy was willing to underwrite the family's living expenses. Although money from Peggy's family had always provided certain amenities not otherwise available to an artist of Crawford's means, such as a separate studio for his work and boarding school for his two sons from this second marriage, Crawford had always resisted living in a style far beyond his income. But in 1960, Peggy's wish that they rent larger accommodations in their Gramercy Park apartment building had led to a commensurate improvement in their life style. Even before this, Crawford had had relatively expensive tastes. He enjoyed fine wine, tailored English suits, a sports car, and good hotels when he traveled. After the family's Gramercy Park relocation, he allowed himself an even greater indulgence in those activities he felt provided nourishment for his art, foremost among them being travel – done either alone or, occasionally, with Peggy or one or the other of his sons.

With increased travel had come a renewed interest in motion picture photography, which he had first essayed in 1938-39 to record his family, much in the style of home movies. By 1948, his intermittent experiments with the medium had reached a stage of development which he compared to drawings or studies in providing information for paintings.[194] By 1965 he had fully appropriated film as an independent artistic tool, using it both as a self-sufficient form of expression and as source material for his paintings. For example, when he traveled to the Grand Coulee Dam in Washington under the auspices of a Department of Interior program to document water reclamation sites around the country, he carried two motion picture cameras and his ubiquitous 35mm camera instead of a sketch pad.[195]

Crawford approached film in the same spirit as he did other media. Uninterested in narrative development, he sought to create satisfying sequences of abstract patterns and textures. His films thus resembled abstract, "moving photographs" whose durational aspect supplanted the endless exposures with which he had previously attempted to counter photography's "seemingly final quality."[196] The results were extended views of isolated, often closely cropped motifs – the movement of reeds in a New Orleans bayou, a fluttering curtain, water churned up by a ferry (Figs. 132, 133). Structurally, Crawford's emphasis on real-time continuity rather than fast-cuts and editing linked his films to those of Andy Warhol. But whereas Warhol's subjects were the denizens of New York's underground society and his films "representational," Crawford's themes were landscapes or objects, and his treatment abstract.

The time it took Crawford to adapt subject matter from photographs and films into his paintings varied enormously. Sometimes he translated an image into paint immediately; other times it was years before he felt ready to do so. *Torn Signs* represents one of the longest incubations. His fascination with the theme of weathered, pasted-over signs had first been expressed in a 1938–39 photograph (Fig. 134), then in a group of drawings, a film in 1969, and in a number of oils (Figs. 135-38). Even when a painting subject related more specifically to a contem-

129. *Pete and Jack's Barbershop, New Orleans,* c. 1960. Silver gelatin print, 7¾ x 9⅝ inches (19.7 x 24.4 cm). Ralston Crawford Estate, New York.

131. *Seville,* 1967. Silver gelatin print, 13⁹⁄₁₆ x 9¼ inches (34.4 x 23.5 cm). Ralston Crawford Estate, New York.

130. *Untitled (Shadows, Seville),* 1967. Silver gelatin print, 9 x 13½ inches (22.9 x 34.3 cm). Ralston Crawford Estate, New York.

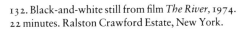

132. Black-and-white still from film *The River,* 1974. 22 minutes. Ralston Crawford Estate, New York.

133. Black-and-white still from film *Torn Signs*, 1973. 5 minutes. Ralston Crawford Estate, New York.

134. *Torn Signs, Philadelphia*, c. 1938–39. Silver gelatin print, 7½ x 9½ inches (19.1 x 24.1 cm). Ralston Crawford Estate, New York.

poraneous experience, Crawford's practice of executing several versions of the same motif meant that his involvement with an image might extend over a period of years. Also, as in the twelve-year execution span of *Boxcars, Minneapolis #2* (Fig. 72), the speed with which an image materialized varied considerably. As he described it to Peggy, "sometimes we have to reach the unconscious with a stomach pump, then sometimes it is like an oil gusher."[197]

135. *Torn Signs #2*, 1967–68. Oil on canvas, 60¼ x 45¼ inches (153 x 114.9 cm). Hirshhorn Museum and Sculpture Garden, Smithsonian Institution, Washington, D.C.

136. *Second Avenue Collage,* 1969. Oil on canvas, 40 x 30 inches (101.6 x 76.2 cm).
Ralston Crawford Estate, New York.

137. *Torn Signs,* 1967. Pen and ink on paper, 11½ x 8¾
inches (29.2 x 22.2 cm). Ralston Crawford Estate,
New York.

138. *Torn Signs*, 1974. Oil on canvas, 54 x 72 inches (137.2 x 182.9 cm). Ralston Crawford Estate, New York.

Crawford's constant travel ultimately began to affect the quality of his marriage, and in 1970 Peggy proposed a separation. Part of her dissatisfaction must have stemmed from his inherently controlling personality and his apparent obliviousness to how it affected others. On one hand, Crawford was a warm, giving person with a playful, ironic wit. He could be an engaging raconteur whose appeal was furthered by his resemblance to an English country gentleman (Fig. 139). To those who knew him more intimately, however, he could also be egocentric and demanding. He refused to speak to Richard Allen for six years because

139. Ralston Crawford, 1970s. Ralston Crawford Estate, New York.

he felt Allen was procrastinating on his text for their proposed collaborative book on jazz (see p. 91).[198]   And Edward Dwight, whose friendship with Crawford was deeply valued by both men, recalled the cruelty and lack of concern for the feelings of others which Crawford occasionally directed at those around him, Dwight included.[199] What finally redeemed Crawford for some, apart from his considerable charm and wit, was his unwillingness ever to be without a basic consciousness of art.

This quality became critical during Crawford's last seven years. In the fall of 1971, while visiting London, Crawford discovered he had an advanced case of cancer. He received the doctor's prognosis that he had only a short time to live with the same unflinching tenacity and moral courage that had earlier driven his painting. Rather than submit to what seemed inevitable, he refused to "follow the script" and instead continued to work and lead an active life.[200] Despite a pain so severe it initially made him unable even to walk, he neither curtailed his travel nor abated his quest for new challenges in art. As late as 1976, considerably weakened, he took up etching again, and spoke fervently of wanting to follow up his earlier occasional efforts at ceramics with sculpture.[201] "I don't know how close I am to the accelerated decline. In the meantime my curiosity continues to be an important drive. I look at the blank canvas or sheet of paper and wonder if I can make it interesting."[202]

Far from becoming a recluse, Crawford brought a new dimension to his social activities during these years. Partly out of a need for companionship after his separation from Peggy and partly out of a lifelong attachment to social protocol and formal English manners, he began frequenting a number of exclusive men's clubs in New York, the foremost being the Century Club.[203] While such a gesture was antithetical to most serious artists of his generation, Crawford's investment in the externals of society ran deep.[204]

Catholicism, too, assumed a new richness in Crawford's life. The religion had held great fascination for him since 1945 when he first began reading Francis Thompson, T. S. Eliot, and Jacques Maritain. Catholicism now embodied for Crawford the same combination of beauty, ritual, and profound commitment which had drawn him to the bullfights. He found in its teachings the potential for ecstatic and non-rational experience that had compelled him at sea. Although the residue of his father's strongly anti-Catholic bias prevented him from converting, he nonetheless began attending Mass.

Crawford's sensitivity to the nobility of religious faith drew him with new attentiveness to the religious parades held in Seville during Holy Week. Even on his first visit there in 1955 he had felt a deep awe for the men who carried the floats through the streets and for their capacity to bear a weight far greater than the sum of their individual strengths.[205] At the time, he had correlated this with the ineffable quality in a painting that caused its impact to exceed the sum of its parts. What compelled him now about the *Penitentes* was another quality he sought in art — integration of the intellectual with the emotional.[206] For the remainder of his life, he would focus his pictorial energies on the conical hoods and waving banners which formed the visual analogue to the spiritual meanings he perceived in these processionals (Figs. 141, 142). For example, the large, simplified shapes that visually extend beyond the framed borders of *Blue, Grey, Black* (Fig. 140) contain a grandeur and pictorial expansiveness unequaled in his oeuvre. Exorcised from this canvas was the emotional parsimony which previously had struck certain viewers as limiting the potential of Crawford's achievement. As in *Seville, Semana Santa* and *Seville, At the Cathedral* (Figs. 144, 145), space advances rather than recedes, psychologically sweeping the viewer into a vortex of pulsing, dynamic movement and emotional empathy. The message of unremitting suffering and ecstatic release celebrated in Holy Week so impressed Crawford that he planned, though never had time to execute, a series of paintings based on the fourteen Stations of the Cross.[207]

Joining Holy Week in Crawford's repertoire of themes in his last years was landscape. He had photographed the landscape in the late 1930s with his first camera and had included landscape motifs in his paintings from the early 1930s, but primarily as backdrops for his depictions of Pennsylvania barns. Even after he gave up industrial themes, his subjects remained man-made. Perhaps as a result of his travels to non-industrialized societies, he turned his attention to nature, first in

140. *Blue, Grey, Black*, 1973. Oil on canvas, 50 x 36 inches (127 x 91.4 cm). Ralston Crawford Estate, New York.

141. *Untitled (Seville, Semana Santa),* 1972. Silver gelatin print, 9½ x 7⅝ inches (24.1 x 19.4 cm). Ralston Crawford Estate, New York.

142. *Seville, Semana Santa,* 1972. Silver gelatin print, 9¼ x 13½ inches (23.5 x 34.3 cm). Ralston Crawford Estate, New York.

143. *Hoover Dam*, 1975. Oil on canvas, 40 x 30 inches (101.6 x 76.2 cm). Ralston Crawford Estate, New York.

144. *Seville, At the Cathedral*, 1974. Oil on canvas, 40 x 60 inches (101.6 x 152.4 cm). Ralston Crawford Estate, New York.

145. *Seville, Semana Santa*, 1975–76. Oil on canvas, 50 x 38 inches (127 x 96.5 cm). Ralston Crawford Estate, New York.

his films, and then in photographs. During the last few years of his life he began translating these experiences into oil. His depictions of isolated rocks and shells against open, uninflected backgrounds (Fig. 149) harked back to several drawings of 1939. Moreover, in several paintings Crawford returned to the Synthetic Cubist mode of his 1942-44 paintings (Fig. 143) and to the sparse, simplified forms which marked his Precisionist style (Figs. 147, 148). He wrote to Freeman, "I may go out the same door I came in."[208] As his health deteriorated, he also began printing negatives of earlier and contemporaneous photographs in larger formats (Fig. 146).

146. *Penstock Leaves #1 (Coulee Dam)*, 1971. Silver gelatin print, 9¼ x 13⁹⁄₁₆ inches (23.5 x 34.4 cm). Ralston Crawford Estate, New York.

Crawford's career fared no better in his last decade than it had previously.[209] Happily, his relationship with his last dealer, Virginia Zabriskie, was one of his best. Always something of a ladies' man, he mailed breezy, charming notes to her from around the world, sent her flowers, and even restocked the wine that had been consumed at an after-opening party she gave in his honor. However pleasant, such gallantries had no effect on painting sales, which continued to be almost nonexistent. Deciding that he was financially better off as his own agent, he began in 1975 to sell work directly out of his studio, while simultaneously retaining several dealers outside New York. It was on a trip to Houston to arrange for a show that Crawford became severely ill and was hospitalized. He died ten days later of kidney failure brought on by myelofibrosis, a variant of leukemia. It was perhaps as he would have wished it, for he had been emphatic about not wanting to die in New York or end his days in a rest home.[210] A man of unbounded enthusiasm for the beautiful and positive in life, he refused even in death to surrender to the negative: as he had stipulated, he was buried in St. Louis Cemetery, New Orleans, with a full brass-band funeral.[211]

147. *Feeder Canal, Coulee Dam*, 1971. Oil on canvas, 30¼ x 40⅞ inches (76.8 x 103.8 cm). Collection of Elaine and Henry Kaufman.

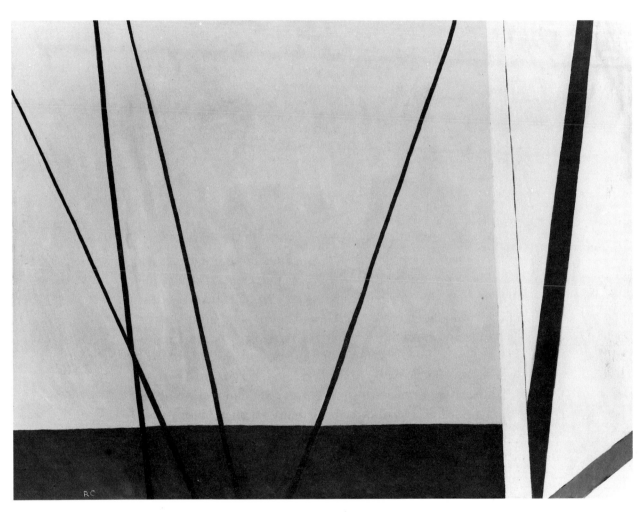

148. *Bora Bora II*, 1975–76. Oil on canvas, 30 x 40 inches (76.2 x 101.6 cm). Ralston Crawford Estate, New York.

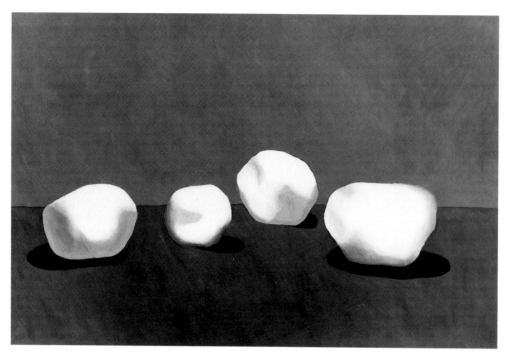

149. *Rocks Near Tarbert*, 1976. Oil on canvas, 30 x 45 inches (76.2 x 114.3 cm). Ralston Crawford Estate, New York.

The steady progress of Crawford's production throughout his life had been a tribute to his faith that the only valid basis by which to judge an artist was the character of his concentration, the quality of the territory he had staked out for himself, and his activity within that territory.[212] He had not painted for money or an audience but out of an uncompromising desire to recognize and perfect his aesthetic territory. Never succumbing to fads or the lure of novelty, he had retained a rare consistency and integrity. From the beginning, his goal had been to synthesize his knowledge and intuition with the discovery and cultivation of his "own garden."[213] "So win or lose I shall in all probability go ahead in my own manner, the solidity of which I constantly examine and try to increase."[214]

Unless otherwise indicated, the repositories of the archival material cited below are as follows: Crawford's letters to Peggy Frank Crawford and Richard B. Freeman, collection of the recipients; Crawford's letters to Edward H. Dwight and Dwight's unpublished essay on Crawford, 1977, collection of Ruth R. Dwight; other Crawford letters, typescripts of lectures, undated notes, etc., collection of the Ralston Crawford Estate, New York (photocopies in the Whitney Museum files). The dates of undated letters and typescripts have been provided by the recipients. Newspaper articles cited without complete data exist as clippings in the Crawford Estate.

1. Ralston Crawford was born to George Burson Crawford and Lucy Colvin. He had two older sisters, Erma and Jessie. A third sister, who also would have been older than he, died at birth.

2. Information on Port Dalhousie and on the shipping career of Crawford's father and uncle courtesy of Mrs. Sheila Wilson, Special Collections of the Saint Catharines Public Library, Marion G. Laskey (a relative of Lucy Colvin), and Blanche A. Scott (a Port Dalhousie resident).

3. Letter to Peggy Frank Crawford, May 12, 1949, p. 4. Crawford was proud that his most palpable childhood recollections were of "the shape of the ships and the harbor"; quoted in Edward H. Dwight, undated, edited transcript of an interview with Ralston Crawford, p. 3.

4. Crawford's father was employed by an American-owned company, the Great Lakes Transit Corporation, and this job presumably motivated the move to Buffalo, just as it had his naturalization fourteen years earlier, on May 25, 1896, in Cook County, Illinois.

5. Information on *The Northern Queen* and its purchase by the United States Shipping Board provided by M. Long of The Great Lakes Historical Society, Vermilion, Ohio; Kathy McGraw of the Detroit Historical Department, Dossin Great Lakes Museum, Belle Isle, Michigan; Teresa F. Matchette, Judicial, Fiscal, and Social Branch, Civil Archives Division, General Services Administration, National Archives and Records Service, Washington, D.C.; and Ardie L. Kelly, librarian of The Mariners' Museum, Newport News, Virginia.
Peggy Frank Crawford, conversation with the author, March 21, 1984, described George Burson Crawford's anti-Catholic bias.

6. For Crawford's years at Lafayette High School, see his transcript, courtesy of Lafayette High School, photocopy in Whitney Museum files. Information on Crawford's performance at Lafayette courtesy of Mrs. Gangloff and Mr. Sheehan of the Office of the Registrar, Lafayette High School, Irvin H. Himmele of the New York State Retired Teachers Association, Inc., Western Zone, Buffalo, and Edward L. Baldwin and Ramsey Tick of the Lafayette High School Alumni Association, Buffalo. Crawford's description of getting honors from U.S. Army "Classification Questionnaire of Warrant Officer," August 3, 1944, unpaginated.

7. For Crawford's arrival in New York, see *Ralston Crawford*, exhibition catalogue (Cincinnati: The Contemporary Arts Center, 1971), p. 2; Peggy Frank Crawford, conversation with the author, March 21, 1984, provided the name of the ship; information on its route courtesy of Richard W. Berry, chairman of The Marine Museum at Fall River, Inc., Massachusetts.

8. Quoted in Edward H. Dwight, undated, edited transcript of an interview with Ralston Crawford, p. 2.

9. Letter to Peggy Frank Crawford, September 8, 1945, p. 6.

10. Eugene O'Neill, *Long Day's Journey Into Night* (ed. New Haven: Yale University Press, 1955), p. 153. Crawford's identification with this passage was noted by Peggy Frank Crawford, conversation with the author, March 21, 1984, and Edward H. Dwight, undated, edited transcript of an interview with Ralston Crawford, pp. 1-2.

11. David R. Smith, archivist of the Walt Disney Archives, Burbank, California, letter to the author, January 13, 1984.

12. Ralston Crawford, letter to Richard B. Freeman, August 13, 1950, p. 2. Freeman, a close friend of Crawford, was his primary public advocate. Until the publication of William Agee's 1983 book on Crawford, Freeman's numerous publications—his 1953 monograph, 1973 book on Crawford's graphics, and his 1962 book on Crawford's lithographs—constituted the primary literature and source material for information on Crawford and his art.

13. Letter to Richard B. Freeman, August 13, 1950, p. 2.

14. For a discussion of The Pennsylvania Academy of the Fine Arts, see *In This Academy: The Pennsylvania Academy of the Fine Arts, 1805-1976*, exhibition catalogue (Philadelphia: The Pennsylvania Academy of the Fine Arts, 1976).

15. Richard B. Freeman, *Ralston Crawford* (Tuscaloosa: University of Alabama Press, 1953), p. 12.

16. For Breckenridge, see Donald S. Vogel and Margaret Vogel, *The Paintings of Hugh H. Breckenridge (1870-1937)*, exhibition catalogue (Dallas: Valley House Gallery, 1976).

17. Hugh Breckenridge, letter to Mr. Myers of The Pennsylvania Academy of the Fine Arts, August 28, 1929, unpaginated, courtesy of the Archives of The Pennsylvania Academy of the Fine Arts, Philadelphia.

18. See the advertisement for The Breckenridge School, in *Eighth Exhibition of the North Shore Arts Association of Gloucester*, exhibition catalogue (Gloucester, Massachusetts: North Shore Arts Association of Gloucester, 1930), unpaginated.

19. Peggy Frank Crawford, conversation with the author, March 21, 1984.

20. The first Breckenridge passage is quoted in Abraham A. Davidson, *Early American Modernist Painting 1910-1935* (New York: Harper

& Row, 1981), p. 244; the second appears in Margaret Vogel, "Hugh H. Breckenridge," in *The Paintings of Hugh H. Breckenridge (1870-1937)*, exhibition catalogue (Dallas: Valley House Gallery, 1976), p. 20.

21. These two facets of Crawford's personality were obvious to those who knew him well; for example, Peggy Frank Crawford, conversation with the author, March 21, 1984, and Edward H. Dwight; the latter, in an unpublished essay on Crawford written in 1977 (pp. 1-2), remarked that "Rally grew up to combine the hard exterior of his father's temperament, with the soft interior of his mother's."

22. Peggy Frank Crawford, conversation with the author, September 4, 1984.

23. Kendall Shaw, conversation with the author, February 2, 1984.

24. Quoted in Jack Cowart, "Recent Acquisition: *Coal Elevators* by Ralston Crawford" (interview with the artist), *The St. Louis Art Museum Bulletin,* 14 (January-March 1978), p. 14.

25. Information about the Horter collection and Crawford's access to it from Horter's former student Albert Gold, conversation with the author, February 7, 1985.

26. For the White collection, see *Philadelphia Museum of Art Bulletin: The Samuel S. White, 3rd, and Vera White Collection,* 63 (January-March and April-June 1968); for the Speiser collection, see *Loan Exhibition of Contemporary Painting from the Collection of Mr. & Mrs. Maurice J. Speiser,* exhibition catalogue (Philadelphia: Pennsylvania Museum of Art, 1934).

27. For a general discussion of Barnes' point of view, see Albert C. Barnes, *The Art in Painting* (New York: Harcourt, Brace and Company, 1937), and William Schack, *Art and Argyrol: The Life and Career of Dr. Albert C. Barnes* (New York: Thomas Yoseloff, 1960).

28. For the first quotation, see the undated (late 1940s), unpublished essay by Malcolm Preston, p. 41, courtesy of Malcolm Preston, Truro, Massachusetts; the second passage appears in Crawford's notes for a lecture at the University of Minnesota, Duluth, May 1, 1961, p. 7.

29. Cf. Gustav Mahler's comment on the fear of compromising originality by looking at other people's work: "If a man eats a beef-steak it is no sign that he will become a cow. He takes the nourishment from the food and that transforms itself by means of wonderful physiological processes into flesh, strength and bodily force, but he may eat beef-steaks for a lifetime and never be anything but a man"; quoted in "The Influence of the Folk-Song on German Musical Art," an interview in *The Étude,* 29 (May 1911), pp. 301-2.

30. Ralston Crawford, quoted in Edward H. Dwight, undated, edited transcript of an interview with Ralston Crawford, p. 5.

31. Quoted in an undated (late 1940s), unpublished essay by Malcolm Preston, p. 38, courtesy of Malcolm Preston, Truro, Massachusetts.

32. Edward H. Dwight, unpublished essay on Ralston Crawford, 1977, p. 5. Dwight wrote that Crawford "went to New York city arriving there during the depth of the depression. He lived near starvation often unable to afford a 5 cent bus ride, but there was a remarkable comoroderie [sic] during these dark days"; ibid.

33. The Tiffany Foundation was established in 1878 to assist unknown artists. Because records from the 1930s are no longer extant, it is not known who recommended Crawford.

34. Edward Alden Jewell, "Art: A Choice of American Painters," *The New York Times,* October 28, 1931, section 7, p. 20.

35. Letter to Edward H. Dwight, October 25, 1952, p. 5.

36. Roger Shattuck, *The Banquet Years: The Origins of the Avant Garde in France, 1885 to World War I* (New York: Vintage Books, 1968).

37. Cercle et Carré was formed in Paris in 1929 by Michel Seuphor and Joaquín Torres Garcia. In response, Theo van Doesburg issued a manifesto entitled *Art Concret* in 1930. Signed by van Doesburg, Carlsund, Helion, Tutundjian, and Wantz, the manifesto signaled the formation of Art Concret. Abstraction-Création was formed in Paris in 1931 as a successor to Cercle et Carré. The group was lead by Auguste Herbin and Georges van Tongerloo, and was open to artists of all nationalities. Important members included Gabo, Pevsner, Mondrian, van Doesburg, Lissitsky, Kandinsky, Arp, Kupka, Magnelli, Baumeister. The group 1940 included among its members Mondrian, van Doesburg, Arp, van Tongerloo, and Taeuber-Arp.

38. John Crawford, conversation with the author, June 8, 1984.

39. See Crawford's comments on El Greco and Goya in his 1935 Fellowship Application Form to the John Simon Guggenheim Memorial Foundation, unpaginated, courtesy of the John Simon Guggenheim Memorial Foundation, New York.

40. Crawford received a B in the class "Teaching of Fine Arts — Advanced"; information provided by Ruby Hemphill, Supervisor, Transcripts and Records, Columbia University, New York.

41. Notes for speech at Student Awards Dinner, Hotel Urbana-Lincoln, Urbana, Illinois, May 23, 1966, p. 6.

42. For the PWAP, see William F. McDonald, *Federal Relief Administration and the Arts: The Origins and Administrative History of the Arts Projects of the Works Progress Administration* (Columbus: Ohio State University Press, 1969), and Richard D. McKinzie, *The New Deal for Artists* (Princeton: Princeton University Press, 1973).

43. The primary criterion for employment on the PWAP for Edward Bruce and George Biddle, who initiated the program, was merit; for others, such as Harry L. Hopkins, administrator of the entire relief operations under whose auspices the PWAP received funds, relief was the goal. The resentment this ambiguity bred was exacerbated in New York by Juliana Force, who initially described the program as a relief measure, only to modify her stand several weeks later by stressing that the selection of artists was to be made on the basis of the best material available. See McDonald, *Federal Relief Administration,* pp. 184, 367, and McKinzie, *The New Deal,* p. 13.

44. "All the marvelous talk about the soul of America, etc., will take on fuller meaning when the painters' check is written. As yet wages in the art projects are outrageously low"; rough draft of a letter to Miss Varga, at *Life,* June 15, 1939, p. 4.

45. In its September 1934 issue, *The New Hope* listed a forthcoming article by Crawford, "The American Renaissance." The October 1934 issue did not contain this article but listed another forthcoming article by Crawford, "The Dealer as Critic and the Critic as Dealer." *The New Hope* ceased publication with this issue, however, before either article could be printed.

46. Information on Crawford's employment records in the PWAP courtesy of Karel Yasko, Counsellor of Fine Arts and Historical Preservation, General Services Administration, Washington, D.C.

47. Some well-known artists received more than $34.00 per week; John Sloan, for example, made $38.50.

48. For a discussion of *Art Front,* see Gerald M. Monroe, "Art Front," *Archives of American Art Journal,* 13 (1973), pp. 13-19.

49. For a discussion of the change in attitude of the American expatriates, see Malcolm Cowley, *Exile's Return: A Literary Odyssey of the 1920s* (New York: Penguin Books, 1969).

50. Quoted in *Art in America in Modern Times,* Holger Cahill and Alfred H. Barr, Jr., eds. (New York: Reynal & Hitchcock, 1934), p. 43.

51. Ralston Crawford, 1938 Fellowship Application Form to the John Simon Guggenheim Memorial Foundation, unpaginated, courtesy of the John Simon Guggenheim Memorial Foundation, New York.

52. Quoted in Crawford's response to a questionnaire, "Treasury Department, Washington, Public Works of Art Project," February 5, 1934, p. 1, courtesy of Karel Yasko, Counsellor of Fine Arts and Historical Preservation, General Services Administration, Washington, D.C.

53. Edward Alden Jewell, "In the Realm of Art: The Independents and Others," *The New York Times,* April 14, 1935, section 10, p. 7.

54. Crawford gave these reasons for his move to Exton in a letter to Henry Allen Moe, Secretary, John Simon Guggenheim Memorial Foundation, October 26, 1935, p. 1, courtesy of the John Simon Guggenheim Memorial Foundation, New York.

55. Quoted in Russell Lynes, "Ralston Crawford," in *Ralston Crawford: Paintings, Watercolors, Prints, and Drawings,* exhibition catalogue (Washington, D.C.: Middendorf/Lane, 1977), unpaginated.

56. Dwight recalled Crawford's mentioning that it was Margaret Stone Crawford's sculpture that graced several Crawford paintings (e.g., Fig. 18); Edward H. Dwight, unpublished essay on Crawford, 1977, p. 8.

57. This was one of the reasons Crawford gave in 1935 for applying for a Guggenheim fellowship; see his letter to Henry Allen Moe, cited above, note 54.

58. See Crawford's letter to Henry Allen Moe, September 9, 1937, courtesy of the John Simon Guggenheim Memorial Foundation, New York.

59. For the American Artists Congress, see Gerald M. Monroe, "The American Artists Congress and the Invasion of Finland," *Archives of American Art Journal,* 15 (1975), pp. 14-20.

60. "Call for an American Artists' Congress," *Art Front,* November 1935, p. 6.

61. The series of exhibitions began with the "First Annual Competitive Exhibition Sponsored by the American Artists Congress," held at the A.C.A. Gallery, New York, June 15-30, 1936.

62. Letter to Louis Lozowick, November 27, 1937.

63. Regarding the resignations from the American Artists Congress, see "American Artists Congress Dissensions – Sundry Other Matters of Moment," *The New York Times,* April 21, 1940, section 9, p. 9. Notwithstanding his resignation, Crawford participated in the Fourth Annual American Artists Congress show which opened one week later; see "Art: Revolt of the Anti-Reds," *Newsweek,* 15 (April 29, 1940), p. 41.

64. Letter to Peggy Frank Crawford, December 2, 1945, pp. 2-3.

65. See, for example, his letter to Henry Allen Moe, Secretary, John Simon Guggenheim Memorial Foundation, November 19, 1934, courtesy of the John Simon Guggenheim Memorial Foundation, New York.

66. Henry McBride, "The Annual Independent Show: Unedited Efforts at Art by the Multitude Again on View," *The New York Sun,* May 2, 1936, p. 18.

67. Ford Madox Ford, "Ralston Crawford's Pictures," *Exhibition of Paintings: Ralston Crawford,* exhibition brochure (Philadelphia: Boyer Galleries, 1937), unpaginated.

68. "Officers Are Re-elected by Art Group at Annual Dinner; Dr. Christian Brinton Returned to Presidency of County Association; Exhibit Opens At Art Centre," *Daily Local News, West Chester, Pa.,* May 24, 1937.

69. For the Research Studio, see André Smith, "Research Studio," *Winter Park Topics;* Jeff Kunerth, "The Once and Future Dream of André Smith," *Florida Magazine,* April 3, 1983; and the brochure for The Maitland Art Center, which the Research Studio later became, courtesy of Ethel Scures, administrative assistant of The Maitland Art Center, Maitland, Florida.

70. André Smith, "Report of President for the Year 1938" for the Research Studio, unpaginated; courtesy of Ethel Scures, administrative assistant of The Maitland Art Center, Maitland, Florida.

71. It is likely that Chanin masterminded the protest; he was dismissed from the colony before the program ended, which fit Smith's description ("Report of President") of a provoker having been thus dismissed. Crawford was probably the cohort to whom Smith re-

ferred in the same report because the two artists had been friends before. Smith accused both artists of having Communist affiliations, although the allegation may have derived solely from their membership in the American Artists Congress; see also "Research Studio Artists in Residence 1938-57"; courtesy of Ethel Scures, administrative assistant of The Maitland Art Center, Maitland, Florida.

72. Smith, "Report of President."

73. Letter to Edward H. Dwight, October 25, 1952, p. 2.

74. 1938 Fellowship Application Form to the John Simon Guggenheim Memorial Foundation, unpaginated, courtesy of the John Simon Guggenheim Memorial Foundation, New York.

75. According to Peggy Crawford, conversation with the author, June 22, 1984, Ralston himself was later wary of drawing analogies between his paintings and photographs for fear of undermining the creative choices of his paintings. However, beginning in the 1950s, he exhibited paintings and photographs together, as in, for example, his 1950 one-artist exhibitions at the Downtown Gallery and the Louisiana State University Art Gallery, and at the Bienville Gallery and Zabriskie Gallery in 1973.

76. Crawford made this analogy in a conversation with Joseph Helman; recounted to the author, May 14, 1985.

77. Quoted in an undated (late 1940s), unpublished essay by Malcolm Preston, p. 39, courtesy of Malcolm Preston, Truro, Massachusetts.

78. Quoted in Susan Fillin Yeh, The Precisionist Painters 1916-1949: Interpretations of a Mechanical Age, exhibition catalogue (Huntington, New York: Heckscher Museum, 1978), p. 11.

79. For Precisionism, see Martin Friedman, The Precisionist View in American Art, exhibition catalogue (Minneapolis: Walker Art Center, 1960); Karen Tsujimoto, Images of America: Precisionist Painting and Modern Photography, exhibition catalogue (Seattle: University of Washington Press in conjunction with the San Francisco Museum of Modern Art, 1982).

80. Quoted in Tsujimoto, Images of America, p. 85.

81. Undated notes for a lecture, p. 7.

82. For example, Crawford preceded Philip Guston (then Goldstein) at the Otis Art Institute by almost three years.

83. Quoted in Tsujimoto, Images of America, p. 85.

84. Rough draft of a letter to Miss Varga, June 15, 1939, pp. 7-8.

85. David Burliuk's remarks were published in a Russian-language article in Russian Voice, February 26, 1939; a similar sentiment about Crawford's work was expressed in Art Digest, 13 (March 1, 1939), p. 23.

86. The identification of the machine with America was widespread in the 1930s. Louis Lozowick wrote, "'Ah, America,' they say, 'wonderful machinery, wonderful factories, wonderful buildings'"; quoted in Joshua C. Taylor, America as Art, exhibition catalogue (Washington, D.C.: Smithsonian Institution Press in conjunction with the National Collection of Fine Arts, 1976), p. 199. And Eugene Jolas wrote in Transition, "America is the leader . . . for on its continent the social

and human structure is ineluctably permeated with the ideology of the machine"; quoted in Taylor, America as Art, p. 187. Crawford's paintings even avoided the wrath of regionalist critic Thomas Craven, who identified America as the land of machines and announced that "the spirit of the frontier . . . is fused and intermingled with the most complicated industrial technology in the history of the human race"; Craven, Modern Art: The Men, the Movements, the Meaning (New York: Simon and Schuster, 1934), p. 270.

87. Quoted in Edward H. Dwight, unpublished essay on Crawford, 1977, p. 1.

88. Peggy Frank Crawford, conversation with the author, June 22, 1984. Crawford's difficulty in separating from Margaret Stone Crawford is also discussed in Dwight's 1977 unpublished essay, pp. 6-7.

89. Robert Crawford, conversation with the author, June 14, 1984.

90. Florence Armstrong Grondal, Stars: Their Facts and Legends (Garden City, New York: Garden City Publishing Co., 1940). Throughout his career, Crawford also found jobs in illustration and advertising; see, for example, his advertisement for the Plymouth Cordage Co. in Time, 43 (January 3, 1944), p. 58, and the jacket for Ruth Darby, Death Conducts a Tour (New York: Doubleday & Co., 1940). In an article in Advertising Agency, he indicated his willingness to make his paintings and photographs "available to advertising"; see Charles T. Coiner, "Clipping Board," Advertising Agency, 46 (February 1953), p. 64. This same willingness to produce commercial work also explains the various record covers he created for jazz musicians.

91. Crawford's average salary for eight months of teaching was $2,000.

92. Letter to the head of the Cincinnati Art Academy, Fall 1940.

93. See Martha Pearse, executive secretary of the American Artists School, New York, letter to Ralston Crawford, October 29, 1936.

94. Quoted in "Artist Finds California Still 'Hinterland' of Art," Santa Barbara News-Press, March 1946.

95. Nora Lee Rohr, Ralston Crawford: Paintings, exhibition catalogue (Buffalo: J. N. Adam & Co., 1942), unpaginated.

96. Richard B. Freeman, The Work of Ralston Crawford, exhibition catalogue (Michigan: Flint Institute of Arts, 1942), unpaginated.

97. The theme of the 1933 Chicago World's Fair was "The Century of Progress"; that of the 1939 New York World's Fair, "The World of Tomorrow."

98. Kootz' letter is quoted and discussed in Serge Guilbaut, How New York Stole the Idea of Modern Art: Abstract Expressionism, Freedom, and the Cold War (Chicago: The University of Chicago Press, 1983), pp. 67-75.

99. Several reviews noted the connection between Crawford's work and that of the geometric abstractionists: Mary L. Alexander, The Cincinnati Enquirer, March 9, 1941; Rosamund Frost, "The Britannica Goes Americana," Art News, 44 (April 15-30, 1945), p. 23. For Crawford's denial of any affiliation with American Abstract Artists, see his letter to Jean Franklin, editor, The New Iconograph, January 27, 1948. On the whole, Crawford tended to reject affiliations with all

groups or movements; see, for example, his letter to the editor, *Art News*, 40 (December 1-14, 1941), in which he dissociated himself from the label "New Realism."

100. Ralston Crawford, "Statements by the Artist," in Edward H. Dwight, *Ralston Crawford,* exhibition catalogue (Milwaukee Art Center, 1958), p. 12.

101. Undated (1946) letter to Peggy Frank Crawford, p. 3. Among the Abstract Expressionists, only Gorky was too old for service. Among the others, de Kooning had no papers; Newman was deferred on physical and ethical grounds; Motherwell had asthma; Pollock was also 4F. In retrospect, the war formed an underlying chasm which separated those who served from those who did not. That the Abstract Expressionists had become prominent during the period when most other artists were in the service confirmed Crawford's resolve to look back on his Army experience as beneficial. It accounted, in part, for his application near the end of the war for a commendation award for his work with the weather service, as if an external symbol of achievement would somehow vindicate his years away from art.

102. Letter to the Selective Service Local Board #10, Cincinnati, Ohio, February 12, 1942.

103. See Jack Cowart, "Recent Acquisition: *Coal Elevators* by Ralston Crawford" (interview with the artist), *The St. Louis Art Museum Bulletin,* 14 (January-March 1978), p. 15.

104. Russell Lynes, transcript of "Comments on Ralston Crawford," Ralston Crawford Memorial Gathering, Whitney Museum of American Art, January 29, 1945, p. 1; Whitney Museum files.

105. Letter to Peggy Frank Crawford, November 25, 1945, p. 4.

106. Letter to Edward H. Dwight, October 25, 1952, p. 4: "Knowledge of destruction as a principal fact of our time was not new to me in the mid-forties, but I wish to say that *my* near destruction in the 40's at Fort George G. Meade and similar places certainly fortified that fact."

107. See "Art: Abstractions and Weather," *Newsweek,* 23 (January 17, 1944), p. 91; see also the brochure published by the Downtown Gallery, New York, for its exhibition "Ralston Crawford: In Peace and in War," January 4-29, 1944, with text by D. N. Yates.

108. Undated (May 1945) letter to Richard B. Freeman, p. 1.

109. See Crawford's memorandum to Colonel Cordes Tiemann, October 30, 1944, and Alva W. Goldsmith, letter to Senator Robert A. Taft, April 24, 1945.

110. Roselle and Stuart Davis, letter to Ralston Crawford, August 13, 1942.

111. The Miller commission came about through the efforts of Burton Tremaine, the owner of the Miller Lighting Company, which had been hired by the Curtiss Wright Company to install fourteen miles of continuous lighting in their aircraft plant in Buffalo. Wanting to advertise what was then a revolutionary lighting system, Tremaine and his future wife, Emily, both art devotees, decided to commission a painting of the newly illuminated plant. It was the reproduction of *Overseas Highway* in *Life* that drew the Tremaines to Crawford, whom they contacted through the Downtown Gallery; Burton and Emily Tremaine, conversation with the author, January 8, 1985. See also Crawford's letters to Burton Tremaine (March 13, 1945, and August 24, 1945) about the commission, in which he also articulated many of his attitudes toward art.

For the *Fortune* article on weather, see "Thunder Over the North Atlantic: New Weather Stations, Improved Forecasting Techniques, and a Squadron of Men Direct the Planes Through the Winds, Ice, and Clouds of Northern Storms," *Fortune,* 30 (November 1944), pp. 154-55, 157, 159.

112. The following discussion is drawn from Crawford's letter to Peggy Frank Crawford, September 8, 1945.

113. Crawford's family had been devout churchgoers. His aunt had been a Sunday-school teacher and, at age three, Crawford had been signed up in the "Cradle Roll Department" of the Presbyterian Church Sunday School. "Cradle Roll Certificate," dated February 13, 1909.

114. Notes for lecture at the University of Minnesota, Duluth, May 1, 1961, p. 12.

115. Letter to Bill Stamper, March 19, 1946, pp. 4-5: "My reaction to the jews in the ovens and endless beyond-hideous procedures of the last few years is an increased sense of my personal obligation to do something solid. I approach my work with a deep sense of this responsibility. If it has only a small note in a positive good direction, then I have justified my existence."

116. Letter to Peggy Frank Crawford, December 6, 1945, p. 16. Crawford reiterated the inadequacy of the rationalist approach in "Artist Finds California Still 'Hinterland' of Art," *Santa Barbara News-Press,* March 1946.

117. For the atomic bomb test, see Oscar E. Anderson, Jr. and Richard G. Hewlett, *The New World, 1939-1946* (University Park: Pennsylvania State University Press, 1962), pp. 580-81; W. A. Shurcliff, *Bombs at Bikini: The Official Report of Operation Crossroads* (New York: Wm. H. Wise & Co., 1947); and William Lawrence, "Atom Bomb Exploded over Bikini Fleet; 2 Ships Are Sunk; Blast Force Seems Less Than Expected," *The New York Times,* July 1, 1946, p. 1.

118. *Fortune,* 30 (November 1944), cover and weather maps, pp. 154-55, 157, 159; 31 (April 1945), cover; 32 (October 1945), cover and weather maps, p. 145.

119. Letter to Edward H. Dwight, November 5, 1947, p. 1.

120. Letter to Deborah Calkins of *Fortune,* May 14, 1946, p. 1: "There is also the matter of considering certain phenomena that will not be directly observed at Bikini. The character of the radioactive particles carried aloft in the atmosphere and moving with air currents will give new and concrete information concerning globular movements of air currents. . . ."

121. Undated (1946) letter to Peggy Frank Crawford, p. 1.

122. Undated (Fall 1949) letter to Peggy Frank Crawford, p. 13: "Then there was a new tack – the Bikini pictures. This was for me very

important, but an aside, in a way. It was food for many pictures – pictures that have never been painted."

123. See *Ralston Crawford: Paintings of Operation Crossroads at Bikini*, exhibition brochure (New York: The Downtown Gallery, 1946), unpaginated.

124. See, for example, "Reviews & Previews: Ralston Crawford," *Art News*, 45 (December 1946), p. 42.

125. Carlyle Burrows, "Imaginative Art," *New York Herald Tribune*, December 8, 1946, section 5, p. 10; Ad Reinhardt, "How to Look at Three Current Shows," *PM*, December 15, 1946, magazine section, p. 12.

126. Marion Summers, "Art Today: Bikini Atoll to Abstraction," *New York Daily Worker*, December 12, 1946, p. 11.

127. See Jeffrey Weiss, "Science and Primitivism: A Fearful Symmetry in the Early New York School," *Arts Magazine*, 57 (March 1983), p. 84; and Kirk Varnedoe, "Abstract Expressionism," in William Rubin, ed., *"Primitivism" in 20th Century Art: Affinity of the Tribal and the Modern*, exhibition catalogue (New York: The Museum of Modern Art, 1984), pp. 615-59.

128. The works in the exhibition "Advancing American Art" were purchased by the State Department in 1946; by 1947 criticism was voiced in Congress; see Margaret Lynne Ausfeld, *Advancing American Art: Politics and Aesthetics in the State Department Exhibition, 1946-48*, exhibition catalogue (Alabama: Montgomery Museum of Fine Arts, 1984).

129. The exchange between Benton and Stefan was reported in *Newsweek*, "National Affairs: House: Out of the Picture," 29 (May 12, 1947), p. 33.

130. J. C. Briggs and Dameron H. Williams, "Letters: Enigmas," *Newsweek*, 29 (June 2, 1947), p. 6.

131. Letter to Bill Stamper, March 19, 1946, p. 3: "As I walked away from the bldg. in which I got my final papers, I felt like one leaving Leavenworth. The trap had been sprung, but I'd been in the trap so long! I'd learned how to live there! Living out of the trap seems strange."

132. Letter to Moholy-Nagy, late April 1946. Crawford asked to enroll in the Institute on a "quite informal basis" to study "photography, still and motion, as well as some typographic procedure." Moholy-Nagy countered by asking Crawford to teach drawing and color at the school's June-August session. In the end, Crawford neither attended the Institute nor taught there.

133. Crawford confessed in an undated (1947) letter to Peggy Frank Crawford that "I feel encouraged. For a long time I did not want to admit the moral damage that the army had done to me. It was never a matter of 'going back' to 1942. But it was necessary to reclaim many values and ideas that went in storage, and *stayed there* until 1946."

134. Undated (Fall 1949) letter to Peggy Frank Crawford, p. 14.

135. In an undated (1948) letter to Peggy Frank Crawford, p. 6, he stated: "Never have I felt lower about my work than I did at times this winter. I really mean to speak of my questioning its purpose." In a letter to Richard B. and Barbara Freeman, August 23, 1948, he wrote: "I therefore say that I *never* questioned the statement that I could make pictures. I never had any indecision or even choice. I felt (and still do) that I was a painter."

136. Undated (1948) letter to Peggy Frank Crawford, pp. 6-7.

137. Quoted in "Art: Questions & Answers," *Time*, 58 (April 11, 1949), p. 57.

138. Quoted in "A Modern Artist Explains the Relationship Between His Photography and Painting," *Modern Photography*, 13 (September 1949), p. 77.

139. Lloyd Goodrich, conversation with the author, May 10, 1985. See also Goodrich, *Three Centuries of American Art* (New York: Whitney Museum of American Art, 1966), p. 102: "This attitude [lack of interest in social content] can be seen partly as a reaction to the disturbed state of the world; in pure plastic creation they [abstract artists] were producing aesthetic order independent of outer chaos – one of the artist's immemorial functions."

140. Letter to Peggy Frank Crawford, December 4, 1945, p. 12.

141. "I have thought about my work and how I can function socially in relation to that work. I've got to go back to prewar training. One must keep in training for his work"; undated (1947) letter to Peggy Frank Crawford, p. 15.

142. Letter to Peggy Frank Crawford, December 4, 1945, p. 14. Crawford stated in a lecture that, "for me, the first thing was, *and is*, to keep in training. This involves, among other things, the right companions. This means limited contact with the bourgeoisie – in any country. Because 'bourgeois,' as one wise Frenchman recently said, means *love of money*. *My* loves and those of any artist are different"; notes for speech at Student Awards Dinner, Hotel Urbana-Lincoln, Urbana, Illinois, May 23, 1966, p. 8.

143. Undated (1947) letter to Peggy Frank Crawford, p. 13.

144. Letter to Richard B. Freeman, July 31, 1962, p. 12.

145. Letter to Richard B. Freeman, August 4, 1946, p. 2.

146. Letter to Richard B. Freeman, October 20, 1948, unpaginated.

147. Undated (Spring 1949) letter to Peggy Frank Crawford, p. 4.

148. Quoted in *Paintings: Ralston Crawford*, exhibition brochure (Santa Barbara Museum of Art, 1946). In a similar spirit, Crawford wrote: "I look to the left and to the right, ahead and behind. Then I paint from my memory and from the thoughts about the things I have remembered. In these recollections the last instant and many years ago are important. Perhaps it would be a difficult synthesis to establish, but a picture referring to Pennsylvania, with further reference to Nanakuli, seems possible to me"; quoted in "Comment on Modern Art by the Artist," *Paradise of the Pacific*, 59 (August 1947), p. 19.

149. Quoted in Russell Lynes, "Ralston Crawford," in *Ralston Crawford: Paintings, Watercolors, Prints, and Drawings*, exhibition catalogue (Washington, D.C.: Middendorf/Lane, 1977), unpaginated.

150. Quoted in H. H. Arnason, "Ralston Crawford," in *Ralston Crawford: Oils and Lithographs,* exhibition catalogue (New York: Nordness Gallery, 1963), unpaginated.

151. Quoted in "Statements by the Artist," in Edward H. Dwight, *Ralston Crawford,* exhibition catalogue (Milwaukee Art Center, 1958), p. 11.

152. Crawford drawing notebook, undated, unpaginated, c. 1951.

153. Ralston Crawford, "Studies in Black and White," *Direction,* 3 (March 1940), p. 21; "Photographs by Ralston Crawford," *Paradise of the Pacific,* 59 (Christmas 1947), pp. 4-5; Ralston Crawford, "A Modern Artist Explains the Relationship Between His Photography and Painting," *Modern Photography,* 13 (September 1949), pp. 74-79, 110.

154. Undated letter to Peggy Frank Crawford, p. 2.

155. Ibid.

156. Undated (1947) letter to Peggy Frank Crawford, p. 4.

157. Ibid.

158. The only connection Crawford had with the Abstract Expressionists was occasioned by the protest held at The Museum of Modern Art on March 5, 1948, "The Modern Artist Speaks," in reaction to the announcement that the Boston Institute was removing the word "modern" from its name.

159. The corollary of Crawford's insistence on the "discovery" that occurred during the act of painting was his criticism of knowing *too* much before painting it: he insisted that "excessive reflection can have a paralyzing effect" and that even drawings, if overly crystallized, could deprive a work of its magic; Ralston Crawford, notes for speech at Student Awards Dinner, Hotel Urbana-Lincoln, Urbana, Illinois, May 23, 1966, p. 8; Jack Cowart, "Recent Acquisition: *Coal Elevators* by Ralston Crawford," *The St. Louis Art Museum Bulletin,* 14 (January-March 1978), p. 12.

160. See "Symposium: Is the French Avant Garde Overrated?" *Art Digest,* 27 (September 15, 1953), p. 12.

161. For Browne and the Kootz Gallery, see Serge Guilbaut, *How New York Stole the Idea of Modern Art: Abstract Expressionism, Freedom, and the Cold War* (Chicago: The University of Chicago Press, 1983), p. 71.

162. Crawford's academic appointments were as follows: summer 1947, Honolulu Academy of Arts, Hawaii; 1948-49 academic year, The Brooklyn Museum Art School, New York; 1949, six weeks at the Art Academy of Cincinnati; spring semester 1949, University of Minnesota, Minneapolis; 1949-50 academic year, Louisiana State University, Baton Rouge; 1951-52 academic year, University of Colorado, Boulder; spring 1953 to fall 1956, New School for Social Research, New York; summer 1953, University of Michigan, Ann Arbor; 1958, University of Colorado, Boulder; 1960-62, Hofstra University, Hempstead, New York; 1960, University of Kentucky, Lexington, and University of Southern California, Los Angeles.

163. James Lechay, conversation with the author, January 1985.

164. Undated (Fall 1949) letter to Peggy Frank Crawford. Crawford repeated a similar view to the Shaws in 1960: "Exhaling without inhaling equals dehydration. Inhaling is difficult if one spends too much time among the students"; undated letter (1960) to Kendall and Frances Shaw, p. 1, courtesy of Kendall Shaw, New York.

165. Undated (1950) letter to Peggy Frank Crawford, p. 3.

166. Letter to Richard B. Freeman, October 16, 1965, p. 1.

167. Ibid.

168. Crawford argued that "certainly pressures exist in this country today that are not conducive to the presentation of a variety of expression from one artist (or even notable variety within large groups). So we find a great deal of uniformity. This is not a virtue, but indicates the use of a formula. Today the trademark is, for many, a mighty important thing, and it affects the attitude of many museum directors, many painters and art dealers who frequently want paintings that can be recognized as the work of a particular artist at a distance of 200 feet"; "Statements by the Artist," in Edward H. Dwight, *Ralston Crawford,* exhibition catalogue (Milwaukee Art Center, 1958), pp. 9-10.

169. Undated (postmarked April 22, 1959) letter to Kendall Shaw, pp. 1-2, courtesy of Kendall Shaw, New York.

170. Quoted in Edward H. Dwight, *Ralston Crawford,* exhibition catalogue (Milwaukee Art Center, 1958), p. 11.

171. Letter to Crawford from Deborah Calkins, editor at *Fortune,* March 21, 1950.

172. Quoted in "A Modern Artist Explains the Relationship Between His Photography and Painting," *Modern Photography,* 13 (September 1949), p. 77.

173. Ibid.

174. Tape of the seminar Crawford conducted at Tulane University for Richard Allen's class; tape on deposit in the Archive of Jazz, Tulane University.

175. Letter to Edward H. Dwight, October 25, 1952, p. 2.

176. Ibid.

177. Charles Sheeler, quoted in "Precision's Reward," *Time,* 79 (June 1, 1962), p. 65.

178. Kendall Shaw, conversation with the author, February 11, 1984.

179. Letter to Edward H. Dwight, October 25, 1952, p. 4; and Ralston Crawford, "Statement," in H. H. Arnason, *40 American Painters, 1940-1950,* exhibition catalogue (Minneapolis: The University Gallery, University of Minnesota, 1951), unpaginated.

180. Undated (May 1945) letter to Richard B. Freeman, pp. 2-3.

181. Letter to Peggy Frank Crawford, December 6, 1945, p. 6.

182. Letter to Edward H. Dwight, October 25, 1952, pp. 4-5.

183. Quoted in *Ralston Crawford,* exhibition brochure (Cincinnati: The Contemporary Arts Center, 1971), p. 4.

184. Quoted in William C. Agee, *Ralston Crawford* (New York: Twelve Trees Press, 1983), opposite plate 46.

185. In a letter to Dwight, October 25, 1952, p. 2, Crawford identified his 1949 lithographs as being about Bikini, but indicated that their specific source was a 1944 drawing he had made illustrating a story in *New Direction*.

186. Letter to Edward H. Dwight, October 25, 1952, p. 5.

187. Letter to Edward H. Dwight, November 5, 1947, p. 1.

188. Quoted in "Artist's Statement," in *Ralston Crawford: Retrospective of Lithographs*, exhibition catalogue (New York: Nordness Gallery, 1961), unpaginated.

189. Letter to Kendall Shaw, December 19, 1954, p. 1, courtesy of Kendall Shaw, New York.

190. Crawford had several one-man museum exhibitions during the 1950s. But as with his extremely well-selected survey at the Milwaukee Art Center in 1958, they generated no national interest. In 1953, the University of Alabama did publish *Ralston Crawford* by Richard B. Freeman.

191. Robert Rosenblum, "Ralston Crawford," *Arts Digest*, 29 (November 15, 1954), pp. 23-24.

192. Emily Genauer, "Whitney Museum to Show Paintings by 'Precisionists,'" *New York Herald Tribune*, January 25, 1961, p. 17.

193. Letter to Richard B. and Barbara Freeman, February 12, 1966, p. 1.

194. Letter to Richard B. Freeman, October 20, 1948, unpaginated.

195. John DeWitt, "Reclamation Launches Art Program," *Reclamation Era: A Water Review Quarterly*, 56 (February 1970), pp. 7-8.

196. Ralston Crawford, "A Modern Artist Explains the Relationship Between His Photography and Painting," *Modern Photography*, 13 (September 1949), p. 77.

197. Undated (Fall 1949) letter to Peggy Frank Crawford, p. 1.

198. Richard Allen, conversation with the author, September 5, 1984.

199. Edward H. Dwight, unpublished essay on Crawford, 1977, pp. 3, 16.

200. Letter to Virginia Zabriskie, May 10, 1975, courtesy of Virginia Zabriskie, New York.

201. Crawford executed two series of ceramics: a vessel series from 1954 in black, white, and blue glaze; the other of pitcher forms in 1960 using grays, browns, and tans. Ceramics in possession of the Crawford Estate.

202. Letter to Richard B. Freeman, March 2, 1969.

203. Crawford's father had had a similar investment in social clubs. When he died, his obituaries listed him as belonging to the Seymour Lodge, F. & A.M., and the Ramses Temple, Toronto; see "Veteran Lakes Captain Dead," *Buffalo Evening News*, May 14, 1937, p. 37.

204. For example, during the war he had refrained from initiating a conversation with one of Peggy's friends at a party because he felt the friend's higher rank might make such an overture inappropriate; Peggy Frank Crawford, conversation with the author, June 22, 1984.

205. Peggy Frank Crawford, conversation with the author, July 6, 1984.

206. Crawford described this as "integration on various levels"; quoted in "Statements by the Artist," in Edward H. Dwight, *Ralston Crawford*, exhibition catalogue (Milwaukee Art Center, 1958), p. 9.

207. John Crawford, conversation with the author, June 8, 1984.

208. Letter to Richard B. Freeman, November 28, 1976.

209. As was true earlier, Crawford's lithographs, photographs, and works on paper generated more attention and sales in the 1970s than did his paintings. In 1973 the University of Kentucky published *Graphics '73: Ralston Crawford* by Richard B. Freeman. In 1974 the Sheldon Memorial Art Gallery, University of Nebraska, published *The Photography of Ralston Crawford* by Norman A. Geske.

210. Letter to Virginia Zabriskie, May 10, 1975, courtesy of Virginia Zabriskie, New York.

211. Crawford had stipulated a brass-band funeral as early as 1956; Kendall Shaw, conversation with the author, February 11, 1984. Crawford, in a copy of his will dated 1956, requested that the Eureka Brass Band and John Casimir's Brass Band perform along with the following individual musicians: Bill Matthews, Louis Nelson, and Jim Robinson, trombone; Albert Burbank and Emil Barnes, clarinet; Thomas Jefferson and Alvin Alcorn, trumpet; and Freddie Coleman and Happy Goldston, drums.

212. Letter to Richard B. and Barbara Freeman, February 12, 1966, p. 2.

213. Letter to Richard B. Freeman, January 27, 1948, p. 3.

214. Letter to Richard B. and Barbara Freeman, August 23, 1948, p. 10.

Selected Exhibitions and Bibliography

One-man exhibitions and selected group exhibitions are listed in chronological order; an asterisk denotes a one- or two-man exhibition. Catalogues are cited within the data on individual exhibitions; reviews and related publications are listed alphabetically by author or title immediately following each exhibition and are indented. Many of the reviews cited were taken from clippings in the Ralston Crawford Estate; when the title of a review is unknown, the first words of the clipping are given. Books and articles unrelated to exhibitions are listed at the end of each year.

1931
Hotel Marguery, New York. "American Painters." Fall (brochure, with text by P[atrick] L. C[odyre]; checklist).

> Jewell, Edward Alden. "Art: A Choice of American Painters." *The New York Times,* October 28, 1931, section 7, p. 20.

> Knowlton, Walter. "Around the Galleries." *Creative Art,* 9 (December 1931), p. 492.

> "Young Americans." *The Art Digest,* 6 (December 1, 1931), p. 11.

Balzac Galleries, New York. "American Painters." November (brochure, with text by P[atrick] L. C[odyre]).

> "Young Americans." *The Art Digest,* 6 (December 1, 1931), p. 11.

1932
Phillips Mill, New Hope, Pennsylvania. "Fall Art Exhibition." October 1–30 (checklist).

1933
Art Club Gallery, Philadelphia. "The Fellowship of The Pennsylvania Academy of the Fine Arts Annual Exhibition." February 9–March 1 (checklist).

Art League of Washington, D.C. "Selected Groups of Miscellaneous Work in Various Media from the Studios of Artists in the Delaware Valley Region, Philadelphia, and New York." March 16–April 7 (checklist).

> "New Hope." *The Art Digest,* 7 (April 15, 1933), p. 11.

Mellon Gallery, Philadelphia. "New Hope Independents" (Henry Baker, McClure Capps, Ralston Crawford, Robert H. Hogue, Peter Keenan, Robert A. D. Miller, Lloyd R. Ney). May 24–June 17 (catalogue).

> "New Hope's Rebels." *The Art Digest,* 7 (June 1, 1933), p. 12.

Independent Gallery, New Hope, Pennsylvania. "Group Exhibition." Fall.

Phillips Mill, New Hope, Pennsylvania. "Group Exhibition." September 30–October 30.

Library Building, Wilmington. "The Wilmington Society of the Fine Arts 20th Annual Exhibition: Delaware Artists, Pupils of Howard Pyle, Members of the Society." November 6–26 (checklist).

1934
*Print Room, The Maryland Institute, Baltimore. "Paintings by Ralston Crawford." January 21–February 4.

The Pennsylvania Academy of the Fine Arts, Philadelphia. "129th Annual Exhibition." January 28–February 25 (catalogue).

Art Club Gallery, Philadelphia. "The Fellowship of The Pennsylvania Academy of the Fine Arts Annual Exhibition." February 8–28 (checklist).

Grand Central Palace, New York. "The Society of Independent Artists 18th Annual Exhibition." April 13–May 6 (checklist).

> "In the Spotlight of the Week's Exhibitions." *The New York Times,* April 22, 1934, section 10, p. 7.

Davenport Gallery, New Hope, Pennsylvania. "New Hope Independents." October 2–29.

> "New Hope Exhibitions." *The New Hope,* 2 (October 1934), pp. 3–4.

"Four New Hope Painters." *The New Hope,* 2 (February 1934), p. 7.

1935
The Art Institute of Chicago. "The 14th International Water Color Exhibition." March 21–June 2 (catalogue).

The Corcoran Gallery of Art, Washington, D.C. "The 14th Biennial Exhibition of Contemporary American Oil Paintings." March 24–May 5 (catalogue).

The Philadelphia Sketch Club. "71st Annual Exhibition of Oil Sketches." April 1–13 (checklist).

Grand Central Palace, New York. "The Society of Independent Artists 19th Annual Exhibition." April 6–28 (checklist).

> Jewell, Edward Alden. "In the Realm of Art: The Independents and Others." *The New York Times,* April 14, 1935, section 10, p. 7.

The Chester County Art Association, West Chester, Pennsylvania. "Fourth Annual Exhibition." May 26–June 9.

The Pennsylvania Academy of the Fine Arts, Philadelphia. "The 33rd

Annual Philadelphia Water Color Exhibition and the 34th Annual Exhibition of Miniatures." November 3–December 8 (catalogue).

Library Building, Wilmington. "The Wilmington Society of the Fine Arts 22nd Annual Exhibition: Delaware Artists, Pupils of Howard Pyle, Members of the Society." November 4–23 (checklist).

1936
Grand Central Palace, New York. "The Society of Independent Artists 20th Annual Anniversary Exhibition." April 24–May 17 (checklist).

> Jewell, Edward Alden. "The 'How' and the 'What': Signs of Our Time Exemplified by Artists of the Salons, Independents, and Others." *The New York Times,* May 10, 1936, section 10, p. 7.

> McB[ride], H[enry]. "The Annual Independent Show: Unedited Efforts at Art by the Multitude Again on View." *The New York Sun,* May 2, 1936, p. 18.

> Sayre, Anne Hamilton. "A Strong Selection in the 20th Independent Show." *Art News,* 34 (May 2, 1936), p. 6.

A.C.A. Gallery, New York. "First Annual Competitive Exhibition Sponsored by the American Artists Congress." June 15–30 (brochure, with text by H. Baron; checklist).

> Devree, Howard. "In the Realm of Art: The Early Summer Calendar with a Distinctly American Flavor." *The New York Times,* June 21, 1936, section 9, p. 7.

Library Building, Wilmington. "The Wilmington Society of the Fine Arts 23rd Annual Exhibition: Delaware Artists, Pupils of Howard Pyle, Members of the Society." November 2–28 (checklist).

Boyer Galleries, New York. "Paintings by David Burliuk, Ralston Crawford, Andrew Dasburg, Emlen Etting, Arshile Gorky, John McCrady, Harold Weston; Sculpture by Chaim Gross, Oronzio Maldarelli." December.

> "Boyer in New York." *The Art Digest,* 11 (December 1, 1936), p. 14.

> R.F. "New Exhibitions of the Week: A Philadelphia Gallery Comes to New York." *Art News,* 35 (December 5, 1936), p. 15.

The Chester County Art Association, West Chester, Pennsylvania. "Fifth Annual Exhibition." December 5–14 (checklist).

The Art Club of Philadelphia. "43rd Annual Exhibit of Oil Paintings." December 5, 1936–January 9, 1937 (checklist).

1937
Art Club Gallery, Philadelphia. "The Fellowship of The Pennsylvania Academy of the Fine Arts, Annual Exhibition." February 4–24 (checklist).

*Boyer Galleries, Philadelphia. "Exhibition of Paintings: Ralston Crawford" (paintings and drawings). March 10–30 (brochure, with text by Ford Madox Ford; checklist).

> Bonte, C. H. "An almost geometrical rigidity of outline,

simplicity of design. . . ." *The Philadelphia Inquirer,* March 14, 1937.

> "Crawford Simplicity." *The Art Digest,* 11 (April 1, 1937), p. 11.

> Grafly, Dorothy. "Boyer Galleries." *Philadelphia Record,* March 14, 1937.

Grand Central Palace, New York. "The Society of Independent Artists 21st Annual Anniversary Exhibition." April 2–25 (checklist).

The Art Centre, West Chester, Pennsylvania. "The Chester County Art Association Sixth Annual Exhibition." May 23–June 6 (checklist).

Boyer Galleries, New York. "Modern American Paintings" (David Burliuk, Ralston Crawford, Arshile Gorky, John Kane, Alfred Mauer, Harold Weston). To June 15.

> Devree, Howard. "And Still They Come – Late Season Exhibitions in the Galleries Vie with Shows Designed for Doldrums." *The New York Times,* June 13, 1937, section 11, p. 7.

Boyer Galleries, New York. "American Pictures" (David Burliuk, George Constant, Ralston Crawford, Emlen Etting, Herman Maril, Harold Weston). August.

> "American Pictures." *New York Herald Tribune,* August 22, 1937, section 7, p. 6.

Whitney Museum of American Art, New York. "Annual Exhibition of Contemporary American Painting." November 10–December 12 (catalogue).

*Boyer Galleries, Philadelphia. "Recent Paintings by Ralston Crawford." December 7–27 (checklist).

> Grafly, Dorothy. "Boyer Galleries." *Philadelphia Record,* December 12, 1937.

> Lewis, Edward R. "Deified Geometry." *The Philadelphia Inquirer,* December 12, 1937.

1938
The Society of the Four Arts, Palm Beach. "An Exhibition by the Artists of Florida." April 3–17 (checklist).

Grand Central Palace, New York. "The Society of Independent Artists 22nd Annual Exhibition." April 28–May 18 (checklist).

> Davidson, Martha. "'Independents' Annual Spring Gambol: Come One, Come All Proves a Questionable Basis for a Show." *Art News,* 36 (May 7, 1938), p. 15.

A.C.A. Galleries, Philadelphia. "Group Exhibition." September.

> "Crawford Shows Art." *The Wilmington Journal – Every Evening,* September 24, 1938.

> Lewis, Edward R. "9 Young Painters in Group Show." *The Philadelphia Inquirer,* September 18, 1938.

*The Philadelphia Art Alliance. "Ralston Crawford" (paintings). December 14–24 (brochure, with text by Ford Madox Ford, excerpted from 1937 Boyer Galleries, Philadelphia, exhibition brochure).

Grafly, Dorothy. "Westcott and Crawford." *Philadelphia Record,* December 18, 1938.

Harris, Ruth Green. "In the Realm of Art: Activities Before the Holidays." *The New York Times,* December 18, 1938, p. 11.

Lewis, Edward R. "Crawford Culls Simplicity." *The Philadelphia Inquirer,* December 18, 1938.

Richter, Jane. "Art of the Month." *Arts in Philadelphia,* 1 (January 1939), pp. 16–17.

1939

Clearwater Art Museum, Florida. "Third Annual Exhibition, Contemporary Oil Painting." January 4–25 (checklist).

Palace of Fine Arts, San Francisco. "Golden Gate International Exposition, Contemporary Art." Opened February 18 (catalogue).

"Director Treks 30,000 Miles to Get Best of U.S. Art for Golden Gate Fair." *Life,* 6 (February 13, 1939), p. 37.

McKinney, Roland J. "American Art at San Francisco." *Magazine of Art,* 32 (March 1939), p. 162.

"San Francisco Presents One Man's Opinion of Living American Art." *The Art Digest,* 13 (March 15, 1939), pp. 30–31.

*Boyer Galleries, New York. "Ralston Crawford: Paintings." February 23–March 11 (brochure, with text by Weldon Bailey; checklist).

"Art: He-Men of the Easel." *Newsweek,* 13 (March 6, 1939), p. 35.

Burrows, Carlyle. "Notes & Comments in Events on Art: Ralston Crawford." *New York Herald Tribune,* March 5, 1939, section 6, p. 8.

"Crawford's Abstractions." *The Art Digest,* 13 (March 1, 1939), p. 23.

Devree, Howard. "A Reviewer's Notebook: Paintings by Modernists Among Recently Opened Exhibitions in the Galleries." *The New York Times,* March 5, 1939, section 10, p. 10.

Gregory, K. "Art." *Town & Country,* 94 (February 1939), p. 66.

Holme, Bryan. "New York: Ralston Crawford." *The Studio,* 117 (May 1939), p. 229.

Klein, Jerome. "Native Artists Are Featured in Shows of Week: Crawford at Boyer." *New York Post,* March 11, 1939, p. 5.

McB[ride], H[enry]. "Attractions in the Galleries." *The New York Sun,* March 4, 1939, p. 14.

McCausland, Elizabeth. "Gallery Index: Boyer Galleries." *Parnassus,* 11 (March 1939), p. 34.

"New Exhibitions of the Week: Crawford at Boyer Galleries." *Art News,* 37 (March 4, 1939), p. 21.

New York World's Fair. "Exhibition of Contemporary American Art." April 30–October (catalogue).

Bear, Donald J. "American Art Today." *The Art Digest,* 13 (June 1, 1939), p. 24.

McCausland, Elizabeth. "Living American Art." *Parnassus,* 11 (May 1939), p. 18.

Boyer Galleries, New York. "Modern American Paintings." June 5–30 (checklist).

"Hogue to Burliuk." *The Art Digest,* 13 (June 1, 1939), p. 45.

Cincinnati Art Museum. "The 46th Annual Exhibition of American Art." October 7–November 5 (catalogue).

Boyer Galleries, New York. "Watercolor Exhibition by 15 Americans." To December 9 (checklist).

1940

785 Fifth Avenue, New York. "American Artists Congress Fourth Annual Membership Exhibition, Art in Democracy." April 5–28 (catalogue).

Willard Straight Hall, Cornell University, Ithaca. "Spring Art Exhibition." May 19–June 3 (checklist).

Cincinnati Art Museum. "The 47th Annual Exhibition of American Art." November 2–December 1 (catalogue).

Whitney Museum of American Art, New York. "Annual Exhibition of Contemporary American Painting." November 27, 1940–January 8, 1941 (catalogue).

Sacartoff, Elizabeth. "News of Art." *PM,* December 1, 1940, pp. 58–59.

"Whitney Museum Opens Its Best and Largest Painting Annual." *The Art Digest,* 15 (December 1, 1940), pp. 5–6.

Crawford, Ralston. "Studies in Black and White." *Direction,* 3 (March 1940), p. 21. Photographs of a Southern prison.

1941

Cincinnati Art Museum. "A New Realism: Crawford, Demuth, Spencer, Sheeler." March 12–April 7 (catalogue, with text by Elizabeth Sacartoff and statements by the artists).

Alexander, Mary L. "One of the most interesting developments of the past year. . . ." *The Cincinnati Enquirer,* March 9, 1941.

————. "A new realism as envisaged by the Modern Art Society. . . ." *The Cincinnati Enquirer,* March 12, 1941.

Crawford, Ralston. "Editor's Letters." *Art News,* 40 (December 1–14, 1941), p. 4.

Holme, Bryan. "Commentary: Realism in Art." *The Studio,* 122 (August 1941), pp. 50, 52.

"The most amazing feature of the now waning season. . . ." *The Cincinnati Enquirer,* March 30, 1941.

The Corcoran Gallery of Art, Washington, D.C. "The 17th Biennial Exhibition of Contemporary American Oil Paintings." March 23–May 4 (catalogue).

The Cincinnati Modern Art Society, Lending Gallery of Local Art. "Group Exhibition." April (catalogue, with statements by the artists).

Cincinnati Art Museum. "The 48th Annual Exhibition of American Art." November 8–December 7 (catalogue).

Flint Institute of Arts, Michigan. "Art Marches On!" November 14–December 31 (catalogue, with text by Richard B. Freeman).

 "Art Marches on to Michigan: Flint's New Gallery." *Art News* 40 (December 1–14, 1941), p. 30.

 "Distinguished Guests Praise Art Institute: Both Building and Dedicatory Exhibition Lauded." *The Flint Journal*, November 15, 1941.

 Rohr, Nora Lee. "Crawford Honored." *Buffalo Evening News*, December 6, 1941.

Freeman, Norine. "Abstract Art Just Starting to Live, Teacher Declares." *The Cincinnati Post*, April 10, 1941.

1942
The Cincinnati Modern Art Society and the Flint Institute of Arts. "25 Creative American Painters." March-April (catalogue, with text by Peggy Frank and Richard B. Freeman). Traveled.

*J. N. Adam & Co., Buffalo. "Ralston Crawford: Paintings." May 25–June 4 (brochure, with text by Nora Lee Rohr; checklist).

 Rohr, Nora Lee. "Crawford Achieves a New Realism." *Buffalo Evening News*, May 29, 1942.

*Flint Institute of Arts, Michigan. "The Work of Ralston Crawford" (paintings, prints, drawings). June 10–July (brochure, with text by Richard B. Freeman; checklist).

 Huber, Elaine. "One-Man Show at Art Institute Features Clean-Cut Precision." *The Flint Journal*, June 12, 1942.

 Ruth, Helen. "Strong Color Invades Exhibit Displayed in Art Institute." *Flint News-Advertiser*, June 12, 1942.

*The Closson Galleries, Cincinnati. "Exhibition of Paintings by Ralston Crawford." November 2–17 (checklist).

 Alexander, Mary L. "At the Docks." *The Cincinnati Enquirer*, November 2, 1942.

The Metropolitan Museum of Art, New York. "Artists for Victory: An Exhibition of Contemporary American Art." December (catalogue; picture book of the prizewinners).

1943
*Artists' Gallery, Philip Ragan Associates, Philadelphia. "Paintings by Ralston Crawford." March 5–April 3 (brochure, with text by Richard B. Freeman, excerpted from 1942 Flint Institute of Arts, Michigan, exhibition brochure; checklist).

 "What the Artists Are Doing: Crawford Solo." *Art News*, 42 (March 15–31, 1943), p. 21.

The Cincinnati Modern Art Society, Cincinnati Art Museum. "Form and Formula." March 20–April 12 (brochure, with text by Marion R. Becker; checklist).

The Downtown Gallery, New York. "The Third War Loan Exhibition: Crawford, Guglielmi, Levine, Lewandowski, Siporin." September–October 4.

 "The Passing Shows: The Third War Loan Exhibition." *Art News*, 42 (October 1–14, 1943), p. 30.

The Downtown Gallery, New York. "American Art 1943: New Paintings and Sculpture by Leading American Artists 18th Annual Exhibition." October 5–30 (checklist).

Carnegie Institute, Pittsburgh. "Painting in the United States." October 14–December 12 (catalogue).

 B[oswell, Jr.], P[eyton]. "Carnegie Presents Cross-Section of Painting in the United States." *The Art Digest*, 18 (October 15, 1943), p. 30.

 Frost, Rosamund. "The Carnegie National 1943." *Art News*, 42 (October 15–31, 1943), p. 20.

The Phillips Memorial Gallery, Washington, D.C. "Paintings by Artists of Washington, Baltimore, and Vicinity." December 5, 1943–January 4, 1944.

 Watson, Jane. "A Number of Newcomers." *The Washington Post*, December 12, 1943.

George, Major Joseph J. "European Weather." *Air Force*, 26 (June 1943), pp. 20–21. Weather charts by Ralston Crawford.

Kootz, Samuel M. *New Frontiers in American Painting*. New York: Hastings House, 1943.

1944
*The Downtown Gallery, New York. "Ralston Crawford: In Peace and in War" (paintings and drawings). January 4–29 (brochure, with text by Col. D. N. Yates; checklist).

 "Art: Abstractions and Weather." *Newsweek*, 23 (January 17, 1944), p. 91.

 Burrows, Carlyle. "The Paintings by Master Sergeant Ralston Crawford." *New York Herald Tribune*, January 16, 1944, section 4, p. 5.

 Coates, Robert M. "The Art Galleries: Fifty Years Too Soon." *The New Yorker*, 19 (January 15, 1944), pp. 54–55.

 F[rost], R[osamund]. "Crawford: The Air in Abstract." *Art News*, 42 (January 15–31, 1944), p. 20.

 Genauer, Emily. "New Exhibits Show War's Effect on Artists: Crawford's Weather Subjects." *New York World-Telegram*, January 15, 1944, p. 6.

H[arris], M. T[jader]. "Recent Work by M/Sgt. Ralston Crawford." *Direction,* 7 (February-March 1944), p. 25.

Jewell, Edward Alden. "Art: Europeans and Some Americans—Toward the 'Absolute.'" *The New York Times,* January 9, 1944, section 2, p. 7.

_____. "Weather Pictures Make Novel Show: Downtown Gallery Displays Work of Ralston Crawford, Air Forces Sergeant." *The New York Times,* January 7, 1944, p. 15.

McCausland, Elizabeth. "Development of Art as a Social Asset: Pressure of Contemporary History to Evaluate Function – Sergt. Crawford's 'Visual Presentation' for the Weather Information Bureau of the Army Air Forces – His Earlier Paintings." *The Springfield* (Massachusetts) *Sunday Union and Republican,* January 2, 1944.

Riley, Maude Kemper. "Art Exhibitions: To Convey an Idea." *Cue,* 13 (January 15, 1944), p. 15.

_____. "The Artist and the Meteorologist." *The Art Digest,* 18 (January 15, 1944), p. 9.

Watson, Jane. "Another artist now residing in Washington. . . ." *The Washington Post,* January 16, 1944.

The Pennsylvania Academy of the Fine Arts, Philadelphia. "139th Annual Exhibition of Painting and Sculpture." January 23–February 27 (catalogue).

Grafly, Dorothy. "The Penn Academy Comes Up for Air: Handpicking, Accent on Locals Revivifies America's Veteran Annual." *Art News,* 42 (February 1–14, 1944), p. 10.

San Francisco Museum of Art. "Abstract and Surrealist Art in the United States." Opened at the Cincinnati Art Museum, February 8–March 12 (catalogue, with text by Sidney Janis). Traveled.

Janis, Sidney. *Abstract & Surrealist Art in America.* New York: Raynal & Hitchcock, 1944.

*Wesleyan University, Middletown, Connecticut. "Ralston Crawford" (weather maps). Spring.

The Downtown Gallery, New York. "New Important Painting and Sculpture by Leading Americans." April 11–May 6 (checklist).

The Downtown Gallery, New York. "American Art 1944: New Paintings and Sculpture by Leading American Artists, 19th Annual Exhibition." October 3–28 (checklist).

L[oucheim], A[line] B. "Brisk and Brighter: An October Opening." *Art News,* 43 (October 1–14, 1944), p. 24.

R[iley], M[aude]. "Some Carry on in Spite of Prosperity." *The Art Digest,* 19 (October 1, 1944), p. 15.

Whitney Museum of American Art, New York. "Annual Exhibition of Contemporary American Painting." November 14-December 12, 1944.

Frost, Rosamond. "The Whitney Does It Again." *Art News,* 43 (November 15–31), p. 10.

Phillips Memorial Gallery, Washington, D.C. "Exhibition of Paintings by Artists of Washington, Baltimore, and Vicinity." December 10, 1944–January 7, 1945.

Crawford, Ralston. "Art Notes." *Maryland Quarterly,* no. 2 (1944), pp. 83–85.

Laffal, Sgt. Julius. "Basics." *Direction,* 7 (February-March 1944), pp. 7–11. Illustrations by Ralston Crawford.

"Thunder Over the North Atlantic: New Weather Stations, Improved Forecasting Techniques, and a Squadron of Men Direct the Planes Through the Winds, Ice, and Clouds of Northern Storms." *Fortune,* 30 (November 1944), pp. 153–60, 197–206. Cover and weather maps by Ralston Crawford.

1945

The Arts Club of Chicago. "Three Contemporary Americans: Karl Zerbe, Stuart Davis, and Ralston Crawford." February (checklist).

*Caresse Crosby Gallery, Washington, D.C. "Ralston Crawford" (paintings and drawings). April 10–30 (brochure, with reprint of 1937 Boyer Galleries, Philadelphia, brochure text by Ford Madox Ford).

Berryman, Florence. "Ralston Crawford's One-Man Show of 'Abstracts' at Crosby Gallery." *The Washington Sunday Star,* April 22, 1945.

Watson, Jane. "First Show by Crawford Opens Here." *The Washington Post,* April 15, 1945, section B, p. 6.

The Downtown Gallery, New York. "19th Annual Spring Exhibition." To May 26.

"New Canvases Blossom in Spring Group Shows." *Art News,* 44 (May 15–31, 1945), p. 26.

The Art Institute of Chicago. "Encyclopaedia Britannica Collection."

"Encyclopaedia Britannica Unveils Its Collection of American Art." *The Art Digest,* 19 (April 1, 1945), p. 38.

Frost, Rosamund. "The Britannica Goes Americana." *Art News,* 44 (April 15–30, 1945), p. 23.

Pagano, Grace. *Contemporary American Painting: The Encyclopaedia Britannica Collection.* With an introduction by Donald Bear. New York: Duell, Sloan and Pearce, 1945.

Crawford, Ralston. "Air Transport." *Fortune,* 31 (April 1945), cover.

Longmire, Carey. "Weather Out of a Box." *Collier's,* 113 (March 10, 1945), p. 19. Weather chart by Ralston Crawford.

"Radar – The Industry: A Clandestine Business in the Billions Was Built on the Work of the Physicists." *Fortune,* 32 (October 1945), cover and p. 145. Weather maps by Ralston Crawford.

1946

The Cincinnati Modern Art Society. "Before and After: Exhibition of Work by Six Veterans." February 1946.

*Santa Barbara Museum of Art. "Ralston Crawford: Paintings."
April 2–May 2 (brochure, with text by Donald Bear; checklist).
Traveled to the M. H. de Young Memorial Museum, San Francisco;
Portland Art Museum, Oregon; and Seattle Art Museum,
Washington.

Bear, Donald. "Ralston Crawford Exhibit at Museum Highly
Praised." *Santa Barbara News-Press,* April 7, 1946.

Fried, Alexander. "Theory Runs to Excess in Art Show." *San
Francisco Examiner Pictorial Review,* May 26, 1946.

"Ralston Crawford Paintings Are Now on Exhibit." *The San
Francisco Monitor,* May 18, 1946.

The Downtown Gallery, New York. "Six Artists Out of Uniform:
New Post-War Paintings by Crawford, Guglielmi, Lawrence, Levine,
Lewandowski, Siporin." May 7–25 (checklist).

Burrows, Carlyle. "In the Art Galleries." *New York Herald
Tribune,* May 12, 1946, section 5, p. 7.

Devree, Howard. "By Groups and One by One." *The New York
Times,* May 12, 1946, section 2, p. 6.

"The Found and the Lost." *Newsweek,* 27 (May 20, 1946), p.
102.

Hess, Thomas B. "Veterans: Then & Now." *Art News,* 45 (May
1946), pp. 44–45, 71.

Wolf, Ben. "Six Artists Return from the War." *The Art Digest,*
20 (May 15, 1946), p. 13.

Community Education Gallery, Washington, D.C. "Eight Artists
from D.C.: Crawford, Evans, Douglas, Love, Brown, Kainen, Radice,
Lemon." November 10–December 4.

Office of International Information and Cultural Affairs, U.S. State
Department, Washington, D.C. "Advancing American Art." Opened
at The Metropolitan Museum of Art, New York, October 4–27
(catalogue, with text by Hugo Weisgall). Traveled.

Briggs, J. C., and Dameron H. Williams. "Letters: Enigmas."
Newsweek, 29 (June 2, 1947), p. 6.

"National Affairs: House – Out of the Picture." *Newsweek,* 29
(May 12, 1947), pp. 32–33.

*The Downtown Gallery, New York. "Ralston Crawford: Paintings
of Operation Crossroads at Bikini" (paintings and gouaches).
December 3–21 (brochure, with statement by the artist; checklist).

"Art: Pat Chaos." *Time,* 48 (December 9, 1946), p. 61.

Burrows, Carlyle. "Imaginative Art." *New York Herald Tribune,* December 8, 1946, section 5, p. 10.

Coates, Robert M. "The Art Galleries: The Artist and the
World." *The New Yorker,* 22 (December 14, 1946), p. 105.

Genauer, Emily. "Bikini Paintings Superb – as Paintings." *New
York World-Telegram,* December 7, 1946, p. 11.

Jewell, Edward Alden. "Melange of Shows." *The New York
Times,* December 8, 1946, section 2, p. 13.

"Letters: Abstract Understanding." *Time,* 49 (January 6, 1947),
p. 10.

"Our Box Score of the Critics: Crawford, Downtown." *Art
News,* 45 (January 1947), p. 46.

Reinhardt, Ad. "How to Look at Three Current Shows." *PM,*
December 15, 1946, magazine section, p. 12.

"Reviews & Previews: Ralston Crawford." *Art News,* 45 (December 1946), p. 42.

Summers, Marion. "Art Today: Bikini Atoll to Abstraction."
New York Daily Worker, December 12, 1946, p. 11.

Wolf, Ben. "Crawford Interprets the Bikini Blast." *The Art Digest,* 21 (December 1, 1946), p. 10.

"Bikini: With Documentary Photographs, Abstract Paintings, and
Meteorological Charts, Ralston Crawford Here Depicts the New
Scale of Destruction." *Fortune,* 34 (December 1946), pp. 156–61.

Genauer, Emily. "Bikini Bombing Effects Going on Canvas." *New
York World-Telegram,* September 7, 1946.

Koch, Vivienne, "Four War Drawings." *New Directions #9.*
Norfolk, Connecticut: New Directions Books, 1946.

1947

*Howard University Gallery of Art, Washington, D.C. "Drawings by
Ralston Crawford." May 2–15 (brochure, with text by Vivienne
Koch, reprinted from her text in *New Directions #9,* 1946; check-
list).

Crane, Jane Watson. "Wreckage of War." *The Washington Star,*
May 18, 1947.

Honolulu Academy of Arts. "Ralston Crawford: Paintings, Photographs, Photograms." July 8–August 3 (checklist).

"Abstract Painter." *The Honolulu Advertiser,* July 6, 1947.

"Crawford Paintings." *The Honolulu Advertiser,* July 13, 1947.

Coleman Art Gallery, Philadelphia. "Five Prodigal Sons: Former
Philadelphia Artists Ralston Crawford, Stuart Davis, Charles
Demuth, Julian Levi, Charles Sheeler." October 4–30 (checklist).

Crawford, Ralston. "Comment on Modern Art." *Paradise of the
Pacific,* 59 (August 1947), pp. 17–19, 32.

Freeman, Richard B. "Artist at Bikini." *Magazine of Art,* 40 (April
1947), pp. 156–58.

"Photographs by Ralston Crawford." *Paradise of the Pacific,* 59
(Christmas 1947), pp. 4–5.

"Ralston Crawford Talks on Work of Local Artists." *The Honolulu
Advertiser,* August 17, 1947.

1948

Crawford, Ralston. "Crawford Dissents." *The Art Digest,* 22 (April 1,
1948), pp. 32–33.

1949

*Cincinnati Art Museum. "Crawford, Cutler" (paintings by Crawford and sculpture by Charles Gordon Cutler). February 17–March 15 (catalogue, with text by Philip Rhys Adams).

> Alexander, Mary L. "Week in Art Circles." *The Cincinnati Enquirer*, February 20, 1949.

> Bell, Eleanor. "Sculptor, Painter in Show." *The Cincinnati Post*, February 19, 1949, p. 6.

The Downtown Gallery, New York. "The Artist Speaks in Paint, Stone, and Words. . . ." April 5–23 (catalogue, with statements by the artists).

> "Art: Questions & Answers." *Time*, 53 (April 11, 1949), p. 57.

> Gibbs, Jo. "The Artists Speak at Downtown." *The Art Digest*, 23 (April 1, 1949), p. 17.

> Loucheim, Aline B. "The Artist Makes Clear His Aims." *The New York Times*, April 3, 1949, section 10, p. 8.

*The University Gallery, University of Minnesota, Minneapolis. "Ralston Crawford" (paintings, prints, and photographs). April 28–May 20 (catalogue).

> Cole, Mary. "Crawford, 'U' Guest Artist, Explains His Credo." *The Minneapolis Sunday Tribune*, May 8, 1949, section C, p. 30.

> "One-Man Show: Crawford at U." *St. Paul Pioneer Press*, April 28, 1949.

*Pfeiffer Library, MacMurray College, Jacksonville, Illinois. "Prints, Drawings, Photographs by Ralston Crawford." October 12–November 1.

Alexander, Mary L. "Academy Guest Gives Views." *The Cincinnati Enquirer*, January 26, 1949.

Callahan, Janet. "Modern Artist Shuns 'Ivory Tower's' Seclusion." *The Cincinnati Post*, January 24, 1949.

Crawford, Ralston. "A Modern Artist Explains the Relationship Between His Photography and Painting." *Modern Photography*, 13 (September 1949), pp. 74–79, 110.

"Painters of Industry: The Landscape of U.S. Production Seen Through the Eyes of 17 Artists, Past and Present." *Fortune*, 40 (December 1949), p. 141.

"Practical Abstract Artist! He Is Guest at Cincinnati." *The Cincinnati Enquirer*, January 31, 1949.

"Spring Term Course: New Slant on Art Due for 'U' Students." *The Minneapolis Star*, March 29, 1949.

"Teaches Advanced Class: Painter Who Covered Bikini Bomb Test at Art Academy." *Cincinnati Times-Star*, January 24, 1949.

1950

*The Downtown Gallery, New York. "Ralston Crawford: Paintings, Drawings, Photographs." January 31–February 18 (checklist).

> Burrows, Carlyle. "Art Exhibits: Ault, Sepeshy." *New York Herald Tribune*, February 5, 1950, section 5, p. 6.

> Devree, Howard. "Art: Reflecting Our Times – Current Shows of Work by Contemporaries." *The New York Times*, February 5, 1950, section 10, p. 10.

> L[a] F[arge], H[enry] A. "Reviews and Previews: Ralston Crawford." *Art News*, 48 (February 1950), pp. 48–49.

> Reed, Judith Kaye. "Ralston Crawford: Plane and Straight." *The Art Digest*, 24 (February 15, 1950), p. 14.

*Louisiana State University Art Gallery, Baton Rouge. "Ralston Crawford" (paintings, prints, photographs). February 24–March 17 (catalogue, with text by James Johnson Sweeney).

> Scudder, Millicent. "Artist Crawford to Offer 3-Week Exhibit in Allen." *The (Baton Rouge) Daily Reveille*, March 3, 1950, p. 2.

> "Work of Bikini Bomb Artist to Be Shown at LSU." *Baton Rouge Morning Advocate*, March 5, 1950.

*Hart Gallery, Duluth, Minnesota. "Ralston Crawford, Prints/ Aristide Pappas, Paintings." December.

> Finberg, Earl. "'Century Makes Pretty Pictures Undesirable': Lecturer, Artist Shows Works Here." *Duluth News-Tribune*, December 3, 1950, p. 10.

Seeley, Carol. "On the Nature of Abstract Painting in America." *Magazine of Art*, 43 (May 1950), p. 166.

1951

The Museum of Modern Art, New York. "Abstract Painting and Sculpture in America." January 23–March 25 (catalogue, with text by Andrew Carnduff Ritchie).

> Krasne, Belle. "The Modern Presents 37 Years of Abstraction in America." *The Art Digest*, 25 (February 1, 1951), p. 21.

The Museum of Modern Art, New York. "Abstraction in Photography." May 2–July 4 (checklist).

> Vincent, John. "A Vital Question." *Photo Arts*, 1 (October 1951), pp. 11, 23.

The University Gallery, University of Minnesota, Minneapolis. "40 American Painters, 1940–50." June 4–August 30 (catalogue, with text by H. H. Arnason and statements by the artists).

The Art Institute of Chicago. "60th Annual American Exhibition, Paintings and Sculpture." October 25–December 16 (catalogue, with text by Daniel Catton Rich).

1952

*Memorial Hall, Hofstra University, Hempstead, New York. "Paintings and Drawings of Ralston Crawford." February 11–21 (checklist).

> Sevcik, Joni. "Paintings of Ralston Crawford Depict Unusual Adoption of Subject Matter." *The Hempstead Hofstra Chronicle*, February 21, 1952.

Cincinnati Art Museum. "Second International Biennial of Contemporary Color Lithography." March 21–28 (catalogue, with text by Gustave von Groschwitz).

The Downtown Gallery, New York. "New Prints." May.

A[shton], D[ore]. "Fifty-Seventh Street in Review: Print Group." *The Art Digest*, 26 (May 15, 1952), p. 18.

Dallas Museum of Fine Arts. "First Annual National Print Exhibition." June 7–August 2 (catalogue).

"À Travers la Nouvelle Orléans." *Le Jazz Hot*, 62 (January 1952), cover, pp. 21–24. Photographs of New Orleans and jazz musicians by Ralston Crawford.

Crawford, Ralston. Introduction to *Photography: Bonge, Dwight, Guglielmi, Siskind, White* (exhibition catalogue). Hempstead, New York: Hofstra College, 1952.

1953

*Clark Hall, University of Alabama, Tuscaloosa. "Paintings and Lithographs: Ralston Crawford." April 23–May 24 (special issue of the University of Alabama *Extension News Bulletin*, 10 [March 1953], with text by Richard B. Freeman; checklist).

Freeman, Richard B. *Ralston Crawford*. Tuscaloosa: University of Alabama Press, 1953.

Walker Art Center, Minneapolis. "The Classic Tradition in Contemporary Art." April 24–June 28 (catalogue, with text by H. H. Arnason).

Whitney Museum of American Art, New York. "Annual Exhibition of Contemporary American Painting." October 15–December 6 (catalogue).

Crawford, Ralston. "Symposium: Is the French Avant-Garde Overrated?" *The Art Digest*, 27 (September 15, 1953), p. 12.

"Ralston Crawford's Photographs." *The Second Line*, 4 (July-August 1953), cover, pp. 1–12.

1954

*Carnegie Hall, University of Maine Art Gallery, Orono. "Ralston Crawford: Color Lithographs and Prints." February 1954.

Dallas Museum of Fine Arts. "Dallas Print Society, National Prize Print Exhibition." July 4–September 12 (checklist).

*Grace Borgenicht Gallery, New York. "Recent Works by Ralston Crawford" (paintings). November 8–December 4 (checklist).

Burrows, Carlyle. "Art: In the Abstract." *New York Herald Tribune*, November 14, 1954, section 6, p. 1.

P[orter], F[airfield]. "Reviews and Previews: Ralston Crawford." *Art News*, 53 (December 1954), pp. 49–50.

Preston, Stuart. "Abstract in Varying Degrees." *The New York Times*, November 14, 1954, section 2, p. 14.

R[osenblum], R[obert]. "Ralston Crawford." *Arts Digest*, 29 (November 15, 1954), pp. 23–24.

1955

*Weyhe Gallery, New York. "Ralston Crawford Lithographs Made in Paris." October 17–November 10.

B.G. "In the Galleries: Ralston Crawford." *Arts*, 30 (November 1955), p. 50.

Devree, Howard. "Two Who Advance: New Lithographs by Ralston Crawford and Color Prints by Adja Yunkers." *The New York Times*, October 23, 1955, p. 14.

————. "About Art and Artists: Crawford's Striking Lithographs Reveal New Possibilities of Medium." *The New York Times*, October 18, 1955, p. 43.

J.K.H. "Reviews and Previews: Ralston Crawford." *Art News*, 54 (December 1955), p. 56.

"The Print Collector: Ralston Crawford." *Art News*, 54 (January 1956), p. 16.

Dwight, Edward H. "Lithographs by Ralston Crawford." *Art in America*, 43 (October 1955), pp. 40–41.

"New Orleans To-day: Some Personal Photographs from the Scrapbook of the Noted American Artist, Ralston Crawford." *Jazz Journal*, 8 (December 1955), pp. 5–7.

1956

*The Cincinnati Modern Art Society, The Contemporary Arts Center, Cincinnati Art Museum. "Ralston Crawford Lithographs." January 6–February 17 (brochure, with text by Gustave von Groschwitz; checklist).

Alexander, Mary L. "Art: Crawford Lithographs Shown in Exhibition at Art Center; Called 'Distinguished Display.'" *The Cincinnati Enquirer*, section 4, p. 16.

*Grace Borgenicht Gallery, New York. "Ralston Crawford" (paintings). November 19–December 8 (checklist).

Devree, Howard. "Art: Distorted Works – Two Personal Painters." *The New York Times*, November 25, 1956, section 10, p. 14.

M[unro], E[leanor] C. "Reviews and Previews: Ralston Crawford." *Art News*, 55 (December 1956), p. 12.

P[ollet], E[lizabeth]. "In the Galleries: Ralston Crawford." *Arts*, 31 (December 1956), p. 64.

"New Orleans Today." *Jazz Journal*, 9 (December 1956), pp. 20–21. Photographs of New Orleans musicians by Ralston Crawford.

"A Selection of Eight New Orleans Jazz Photographs by Ralston Crawford." *Climax*, 2 (Summer 1956), pp. 56–64.

1957

The Brooklyn Museum, New York. "Golden Years of American Drawings 1905–1956." January 22–March 17 (catalogue, with text by Una E. Johnson).

1958

*Milwaukee Art Center. "Ralston Crawford" (paintings, prints, drawings). February 6–March 9 (catalogue, with text by Edward H. Dwight and statements by the artist).

  Fish, Margaret. "Art and Artists: Crawford One Man Show to Open at Center." *Milwaukee Sentinel*, February 2, 1958, section D, p. 4.

  _____. "Artist Explains Relation of Art." *Milwaukee Sentinel*, February 6, 1958, part 2, p. 1.

  G[etlein], F[rank]. "It's Easy to Follow Route of Crawford's Paint Brush." *The Milwaukee Journal*, February 6, 1958, part 2.

  _____. "The World of Art: Industrial Cubism in Crawford's Art." *The Milwaukee Journal*, February 9, 1958, part 5, p. 5.

  "Ties Painting to Bullfights: Crawford Cites Art." *The Milwaukee Journal*, February 7, 1958, p. 12.

University of Illinois, Urbana-Champaign. "Recent American Prints: Third Biennial Invitational Exhibition." February 16–March 16 (catalogue, with text by Lee Chesney).

The Downtown Gallery, New York. "Portrait of a Building." June 9–27.

  S[awin], M[artica]. "In the Galleries: Portrait of a Building." *Arts*, 32 (June 1958), p. 56.

  "Ten Distinguished American Artists Interpret a Masterpiece of Contemporary Construction Art . . . 100 Church Street." *The New York Times*, June 8, 1958, section 10, cover, pp. 2, 6.

  T[yler], P[arker]. "Reviews and Previews: Portrait of a Building." *Art News*, 57 (Summer 1958), p. 17.

*St. George's Gallery Prints, London. "Ralston Crawford Lithographs." June 12–28 (catalogue, with text by the Hon. Robert M. Erskine).

*Grace Borgenicht Gallery, New York. "Ralston Crawford" (paintings). October 28–November 15 (checklist).

  C[ampbell], L[awrence]. "Reviews and Previews: Ralston Crawford." *Art News*, 57 (November 1958), p. 52.

  Preston, Stuart. "A Twentieth Century Harvest." *The New York Times*, November 2, 1958, section 10, p. 13.

  S[awin], M[artica]. "In the Galleries: Ralston Crawford." *Arts*, 33 (November 1958), p. 56.

University of Kentucky Art Gallery, Lexington. "Graphics '58." November 23–December 20 (catalogue, with text by Richard B. Freeman).

1959

The Corcoran Gallery of Art, Washington, D.C. "The 26th Biennial Exhibition of Contemporary American Paintings." January 17–March 8 (catalogue).

Print Council of America, New York, organizer. "Prints Today/1959." Opened September 15. Traveled.

Watson, Ernest W. *Composition in Landscape and Still Life*. New York: Watson-Guptill Publications, 1959.

1960

*Hofstra College, Hempstead, New York. "Ralston Crawford: Paintings and Lithographs." February 1–12 (checklist).

*Closson Gallery, Cincinnati. "Lithographs by Ralston Crawford." February 1–13.

  Yeisler, Frederick. "In Art Circles: Two Exhibits at Closson's." *The Cincinnati Enquirer*, February 7, 1960, section D, p. 7.

Walker Art Center, Minneapolis. "The Precisionist View in American Art." November 13–December 25 (catalogue, with text by Martin L. Friedman). Traveled.

  Friedman, Martin. "The Precisionist View." *Art in America*, 48 (1960), pp. 30–36.

  Genauer, Emily. "Art: It Seems the Good Old Days Weren't." *New York Herald Tribune*, January 29, 1961, p. 19.

  _____. "Whitney Museum to Show Paintings by 'Precisionists,'" *New York Herald Tribune*, January 25, 1961, p. 17.

  Kramer, Hilton. "The American Precisionists: An Authentic American Fantasy Is Defined in an Exhibition Now Touring the Nation's Museums." *Arts*, 35 (March 1961), pp. 32–37.

  Schiff, Bennett. "In the Art Galleries." *New York Post Magazine*, January 29, 1961, p. 12.

Watson, Ernest W. "The Art of Ralston Crawford." *American Artist*, 24 (April 1960), pp. 47–51, 64–66.

1961

*University of Kentucky Art Gallery, Lexington. "Lithographs by Ralston Crawford." April 16–May 7 (brochure, with text by Richard B. Freeman; checklist). Traveled to the San Francisco Museum of Art; the University of Nebraska – Lincoln; the University of Illinois; the Davison Art Center, Wesleyan University, Middletown, Connecticut; Oakland University, Rochester, Michigan; the University of Maine, Orono.

  Amyx, Clifford. "Crawford Exhibit to Remain at University Until May 7." The *Lexington* (Kentucky) *Herald Leader*, April 23, 1961, p. 53.

*Tweed Gallery, University of Minnesota, Duluth. "Ralston Crawford: Retrospective Exhibition" (paintings, prints). May (brochure with checklist).

*Lee Nordness Gallery, New York. "Ralston Crawford: Retrospective of Lithographs." October 3–21 (brochure, with text by Richard B. Freeman, reprinted as part of his *The Lithographs of Ralston Crawford*, 1962; statement by the artist; checklist).

P[etersen], V[alerie]. "Reviews and Previews: Ralston Crawford." *Art News*, 60 (October 1961), p. 13.

Preston, Stuart. "Art: At the Guggenheim." *The New York Times*, October 13, 1961, section C, p. 69.

T[illim], S[idney]. "New York Exhibitions: In the Galleries – Ralston Crawford." *Arts Magazine,* 36 (October 1961), pp. 39–40.

1962
Whitney Museum of American Art, New York. "Geometric Abstraction in America." March 20–May 13 (catalogue, with text by John Gordon).

Crawford, Ralston. Statement in Allen S. Weller, *Art U.S.A. Now.* Lucerne: C. J. Bucher, 1962.

Freeman, Richard B. *The Lithographs of Ralston Crawford.* Lexington: University of Kentucky Press, 1962.

1963
*Lee Nordness Gallery, New York. "Ralston Crawford: Oils and Lithographs." March 12–30 (catalogue, with text by H. H. Arnason).

 Adlow, Dorothy. "Ralston Crawford." *The Christian Science Monitor,* March 27, 1963, The Home Forum section, p. 10.

 T[illim], S[idney]. "In the Galleries: Ralston Crawford." *Arts Magazine,* 37 (May-June 1963), p. 103.

*Montgomery Museum of Fine Arts, Alabama. "36 Lithographs by Ralston Crawford." April (checklist).

*Walker Art Center, Minneapolis. "Ralston Crawford: Photographs of New Orleans Jazz." July 14–August 18.

Whitney Museum of American Art, New York. "Annual Exhibition 1963: Contemporary American Painting." December 11, 1963–February 2, 1964 (catalogue).

Grey, Cleve. "American Prints Today." *Art in America,* 51 (February 1963), pp. 124–25.

1964
Whitney Museum of American Art, New York. "Between the Fairs: 25 Years of American Art, 1939–1964." June 24–September 23 (catalogue, with text by John I. H. Baur).

Museum of Art, Carnegie Institute, Pittsburgh. "The 1964 Pittsburgh International Exhibition of Contemporary Painting and Sculpture." October 30, 1964–January 10, 1965 (catalogue).

Grey, Cleve. "Print Review: New York Panorama." *Art in America,* 52 (April 1964), p. 109.

1965
*Sheldon Memorial Art Gallery, University of Nebraska, Lincoln. "Ralston Crawford Retrospective" (paintings, prints, drawings). February 15–March 14.

"Artist Crawford: 'Feelings Are Part of the Individual.'" *Southeast Lincoln Sun,* 4 (March 4, 1965), p. 1.

"Artist's Many Facets Sparkle." *Lincoln Sunday Journal and Star,* February 7, 1965, section C, p. 6.

Thiessen, Leonard. "Art in the Midlands: Crawford's Painting Talks for Him." *Sunday Lincoln World Herald Magazine,* February 14, 1965, p. 24.

Crawford, Ralston. "Niles Spencer: A Tribute." In *Niles Spencer* (exhibition catalogue). Text by Richard B. Freeman. Lexington: University of Kentucky Art Museum, 1965, pp. 19–21.

Hillman, John. "Sketchbook." *The Crete* (Nebraska) *Doane Owl,* February 23, 1965, p. 14.

1966
*Krannert Art Museum, University of Illinois, Champaign. "Ralston Crawford." February 6–27 (checklist).

Allen, Richard B. "New Orleans Jazz Archive at Tulane." *Wilson Library Bulletin,* 40 (March 1966), pp. 619–23.

1968
*Brooks Art Gallery, Memphis. "Ralston Crawford: Lithographs." March.

 Northrop, Jr., Guy. "Adventures into Art: Ralston Crawford Prints Shown at Brooks." *Memphis Commercial Appeal,* March 16, 1968, section 4, p. 12.

Whitney Museum of American Art, New York. "The 1930's: Painting & Sculpture in America." October 15–December 1 (catalogue, with text by William C. Agee).

 Siegel, Jeanne. "The 1930's: Painting and Sculpture in America – An Exhibition to Change Art History." *Arts Magazine,* 43 (November 1968), pp. 30–33.

*Creighton University Fine Arts Gallery, Omaha. "Ralston Crawford: Retrospective Exhibition" (paintings, prints, drawings). October 23–December 9 (brochure, with text by L. E. Lubbers).

 Wade, Gerald. "Artist Crawford: A-Bomb Has Not Cut Man's Value." *Omaha World Herald,* October 23, 1968, p. 8.

1969
*Bienville Gallery, New Orleans. "Ralston Crawford: Major Paintings and Lithographs." November 17–December 5.

*The Century Association, New York. "Recent Paintings, Drawings, and Lithographs by Ralston Crawford." February 5–April 27.

Blonk, Hu. "Crawford to Paint: How Will Coulee Dam Look in the Abstract?" *Wenatchee* (Washington) *Daily World,* November 14, 1969, pp. 1–2.

1970
Institute of Contemporary Art of the University of Pennsylvania, Philadelphia. "The Highway." January 14–February 25 (catalogue,

with texts by Denise Scott, Robert Venturi, and John W. McCoubrey). Traveled.

American Academy of Arts and Letters and the National Institute of Arts and Letters, New York. "Exhibition of Newly Elected Members and Recipients of Honors and Awards." May 21–June 21 (catalogue).

Dewitt, John. "Reclamation Launches Art Program." *Reclamation Era: A Water Review Quarterly,* 56 (February 1970), pp. 7–8.

1971

*The Contemporary Arts Center, Cincinnati. "Ralston Crawford: Retrospective Exhibition" (paintings, prints, gouaches, drawings). February 24–March 25 (brochure; checklist).

> Findsen, Owen. "Ralston Crawford Retrospective." *The Cincinnati Enquirer,* February 28, 1971, section K, p. 6.

*Lee Nordness Galleries, New York. "Ralston Crawford: Recent Paintings, Plus Selected Major Oils, Gouaches, and Drawings from the 1930s to the 1960s." April 17–May 7.

> Atirnomis. "New York Galleries: Ralston Crawford." *Arts Magazine,* 45 (May 1971), p. 62.

*Zabriskie Gallery, New York. "Ralston Crawford" (paintings, drawings, gouaches). April 27–May 15 (checklist).

> Atirnomis. "New York Galleries: Ralston Crawford." *Arts Magazine,* 45 (May 1971), p. 62.
>
> Campbell, Larry. "Reviews & Previews: Ralston Crawford." *Art News,* 70 (May 1971), p. 12.
>
> Glueck, Grace. "'Once Upon a Time' There Was a Show: Ralston Crawford." *The New York Times,* May 15, 1971, p. 27.
>
> Lanes, Jerrold. "New York: Ralston Crawford." *Artforum,* 9 (June 1971), pp. 88–89.

*St. Mary's Gallery, Lexington Park, Maryland. "Ralston Crawford: Paintings, Lithographs, Drawings, and Films." April.

> "Ralston Crawford: Paintings, Lithographs, Drawings, and Films." *The Lexington Park Enterprise,* April 22, 1971, section B, p. 1.

*The Helman Gallery, St. Louis. "Ralston Crawford" (paintings, drawings). May 22–June 25 (brochure, with text by Barbara Rose; checklist).

> King, Mary. "Crawford Exhibit." *St. Louis Post-Dispatch,* May 26, 1971, section G, p. 3.

Phillips, Joan. "Ralston Crawford Comes Home: Nostalgic Visit by Noted U.S. Artist." *St. Catharines* (Ontario) *Standard,* January 21, 1971, p. 8.

1972

National Academy of Design, New York. "147th Annual Exhibition." February 24–March 19 (catalogue).

United States Department of the Interior, Traveling Exhibition Service, Smithsonian Institution. "The American Artist and Water

Reclamation." September 1972–December 1976 (catalogue, with texts by Lloyd Goodrich and Douglas MacKay).

1973

*Bienville Gallery, New Orleans. "Ralston Crawford: Paintings, Prints, Photographs." January 28–February 16.

> "Crawford Show." *The New Orleans Times-Picayune,* February 4, 1973, section 2, p. 7.

*University of Kentucky Art Gallery, Lexington. "Graphis '73, Ralston Crawford: Retrospective Exhibition, Drawings and Watercolors." February 11–March 4 (catalogue, with text by Richard B. Freeman). Traveled to the National Collection of Fine Arts, Smithsonian Institution, Washington, D.C.

> Lansdell, Sarah. "Art: Ralston Crawford at UK: Linear Is Beautiful." *The Lexington Courier Journal and Times,* February 18, 1973, section H, p. 16.
>
> Johnson, Lincoln F. "Aerial Photos Resemble Abstraction." *The Baltimore Sun,* May 24, 1973.

*Zabriskie Gallery, New York. "Ralston Crawford: Paintings, Drawings, Photographs, and Lithographs." March 3–30 (brochure; checklist).

> Campbell, Lawrence. "Reviews and Previews: Ralston Crawford." *Art News,* 72 (May 1973), p. 12.
>
> Canaday, John. "Art: Okada's Work Is Pleasure to See – Ralston Crawford." *The New York Times,* March 24, 1973, p. 29.
>
> Masheck, Joseph. "Reviews: Ralston Crawford." *Artforum,* 11 (June 1973), pp. 77–78.

*Whitney Museum of American Art, New York. "Ralston Crawford Lithographs." June 21–July 29.

1974

*Sheldon Memorial Art Gallery, University of Nebraska, Lincoln. "The Photography of Ralston Crawford." January 15–February 10 (catalogue, with text by Norman A. Geske). Traveled to Montgomery Museum of Fine Arts, Alabama; Munson-Williams-Proctor Institute Museum of Art, Utica, New York.

Sheldon Memorial Art Gallery, University of Nebraska, Lincoln, "Geometric Abstraction." April 12–May 2 (catalogue, with text by Judith K. Van Wagner). Traveled.

*The Greenberg Gallery, St. Louis. "Ralston Crawford." October-November.

*Corcoran & Greenberg, Inc., Coral Gables, Florida. "Ralston Crawford: Paintings, Watercolors, Drawings." December 1974–January 1975.

1975

Zabriskie Gallery, New York. "Artists by Artists: Photographs." December 2, 1975–January 3, 1976 (checklist).

1976

United States Department of the Interior, organizer. "America 1976." Opened at The Corcoran Gallery of Art, Washington, D.C., April 27. Traveled.

Zabriskie Gallery, New York. "Urban Focus: Photographs by Berenice Abbott, Ralston Crawford, and Ralph Steiner." September 28–October 23 (checklist).

*Zabriskie Gallery, New York. "Ralston Crawford" (paintings, watercolors). November 23–December 11 (brochure, with statement by the artist; checklist).

Kramer, Hilton. "Art: The Modern's New Masterworks – Ralston Crawford." *The New York Times,* December 3, 1976, section C, p. 17.

*Bienville Gallery, New Orleans. "Ralston Crawford: Paintings, Drawings, and Prints." January 5–February 2 (checklist).

Collier, Alberta. "The World of Art." *The New Orleans Times-Picayune,* section 3, p. 6.

Hirschl & Adler Galleries, New York. "Lines of Power." March 12–April 9 (catalogue, with text by James H. Maroney, Jr.).

Russell, John. "Art: When the Belief in Technology Was Ironclad." *The New York Times,* March 27, 1977, section D, p. 23.

Rosa Esman Gallery, New York. "Photonotations II." May 3–June 4.

*Middendorf/Lane Gallery, Washington, D.C. "Ralston Crawford: Paintings, Watercolors, Prints, and Drawings." December (brochure, with text by Russell Lynes; checklist).

"New Art with Paper: It's Torn, Sewn, Crushed . . . Ralston Crawford." *The Washington Post,* December 17, 1977, section D, p. 2.

Simon, Joan. "New York Today: Some Artists Comment – Ralston Crawford." *Art in America,* 65 (September-October 1977), pp. 80–81.

1978

*The Century Association, New York. "Oils, Watercolors, Drawings, and Prints by Ralston Crawford." February 28–April 2 (brochure, with text by Russell Lynes, reprinted from Middendorf/Lane Gallery, Washington, D.C., exhibition brochure, 1977; checklist).

Philadelphia College of Art. "Seventies Painting." April 21–May 20 (catalogue, with text by Janet Kardon).

Cowart, Jack. "Recent Acquisition: *Coal Elevators* by Ralston Crawford." *The St. Louis Art Museum Bulletin,* 14 (January-March 1978), pp. 10–15.

Glueck, Grace. "Ralston Crawford Is Dead at 71; Abstract Painter and Lithographer." *The New York Times,* May 2, 1978, p. 38.

"Obituaries: Ralston Crawford, 71, Painter of City Themes." *New York Post,* May 2, 1978, p. 68.

1979

Heckscher Museum, Huntington, New York. "The Precisionist Painters 1916–1949: Interpretations of a Mechanical Age." July 7–August 20 (catalogue, with text by Susan Fillin Yeh).

Coral Gables Public Library, Florida. "Great Exposures: Photographs by Ansel Adams, Ralston Crawford, Duane Michaels, George Tice." September.

Kohen, Helen L. "Photography: 'Great Exposures' Exhibit Focuses on Quality Prints." *The Miami Herald,* September 7, 1979, section C, p. 8.

1982

Visual Arts Museum, New York. "The Precisionist Vision." February 8–26.

San Francisco Museum of Modern Art. "Images of America: Precisionist Painting and Modern Photography." September 9–November 11 (catalogue, with text by Karen Tsujimoto). Traveled.

Boettger, Suzaan. "San Francisco: 'Images of America – Precisionist Painting and Modern Photography,' San Francisco Museum of Modern Art." *Artforum,* 21 (December 1982), pp. 84–85.

Platt, Susan. "Precisionism: America's Immaculates." *Images & Issues,* 3 (March-April 1983), pp. 22–23.

1983

*The Art Gallery at the University of Maryland, College Park. "Ralston Crawford: Photographs – Art and Process." March 22–May 1 (catalogue, with essay by Edith A. Tonelli). Traveled to The Frederick S. Wight Gallery of the University of California at Los Angeles.

Eisenman, Stephen. "Ralston Crawford." *Arts Magazine,* 58 (December 1983), p. 4.

Nicholson, Chuck. "Photography: Art and/or Process." *Art Week,* 14 (October 29, 1983), p. 11

*Hillwood Art Gallery, C. W. Post Center, Greenvale, New York. "'Oh, Didn't He Ramble,' Ralston Crawford's New Orleans Jazz Photographs: A Cultural Document." March 30–April 20 (brochure, with texts by Judith K. Van Wagner and Richard B. Allen).

Preston, Malcolm. "Art Reviews: Photos of New Orleans Jazz Life." *Newsday,* April 16, 1983.

*Robert Miller Gallery, New York. "Ralston Crawford." November 22–December 30, 1983.

"Album: Ralston Crawford." *Arts Magazine,* 58 (December 1983), pp. 48–49.

Agee, William C. *Ralston Crawford.* New York: Twelve Trees Press, 1983.

Heilpern, John. "Ralston Crawford's Gift of Selection." *Aperture,* no. 92 (Fall 1983), pp. 66–75.

Lawrence, John. "Ralston Crawford: The Photographs." *The New Orleans Art Review,* 2 (May-June 1983), pp. 9–10.

Jordan, George E. "Ralston Crawford: A Remembrance." *The New Orleans Art Review,* 2 (May-June 1983), pp. 10–11.

1984
*Edwynn Houk Gallery, New York. "Ralston Crawford Photographs." April 10–June 2.

Montgomery Museum of Fine Arts, Alabama. "Advancing American Art: Politics and Aesthetics in the State Department Exhibition, 1946–48." January 10–March 4 (catalogue, with texts by Margaret Lynne Ausfield and Virginia M. Mecklenburg).

1985
*Robert Miller Gallery, New York. "Ralston Crawford: An Exhibition of Photographs." January 8–February 2.

Works in the Exhibition

Dimensions are in inches, followed by centimeters; height precedes width. Dimensions for prints are those of the image only. Unless otherwise indicated, all works are in the Ralston Crawford Estate and are lent by courtesy of the Robert Miller Gallery, Inc., New York.

Paintings

Marine with Island, 1934
Oil on canvas, 40 x 32 (101.6 x 81.3)

Vertical Building, 1934
Oil on canvas, 40⅛ x 34⅛ (101.9 x 86.7)
San Francisco Museum of Modern Art; Arthur W.
  Barney Bequest Fund Purchase

Ventilator with Porthole, 1935
Oil on canvas, 40 x 35 (101.6 x 88.9)
Sheldon Memorial Art Gallery, University of
  Nebraska—Lincoln, F. M. Hall Collection

Electrification #2, 1936
Oil on canvas, 36 x 30 (91.4 x 76.2)
Private collection

Worth Steel Plant, 1936
Oil on canvas, 30 x 42 (76.2 x 106.7)
Des Moines Art Center

Steel Foundry, Coatesville, Pa., 1936–37
Oil on canvas, 32 x 40 (81.3 x 101.6)
Whitney Museum of American Art,
  New York   37.10

Buffalo Grain Elevators, 1937
Oil on canvas, 40¼ x 50¼ (102.2 x 127.6)
National Museum of American Art, Smithsonian
  Institution, Washington, D.C.

Ice Plant, 1937
Oil on canvas, 32 x 40 (81.3 x 101.6)
Collection of Mr. and Mrs. James A. Fisher

Pennsylvania Barn, 1937
Oil on canvas, 30 x 36 (76.2 x 91.4)
Brown Group, Inc., Saint Louis

Coal Elevators, 1938
Oil on canvas, 36¼ x 50¼ (92.1 x 127.6)
The Saint Louis Art Museum; Gift of Mr. and Mrs.
  Richard T. Fisher

Maitland Bridge, 1938
Oil on canvas, 32 x 40 (81.3 x 101.6)
Collection of Emily Rauh Pulitzer

Public Grain Elevator in New Orleans, 1938
Oil on canvas, 44 x 34 (111.8 x 86.4)
Cincinnati Art Museum; Museum Purchase

Sanford Tanks, 1938
Oil on canvas, 36 x 28 (91.4 x 71.1)
Collection of Joseph Helman

Watertank, 1938
Oil on canvas, 30 x 36 (76.2 x 91.4)
The Regis Collection, Minneapolis

Overseas Highway, 1939
Oil on canvas, 28 x 45 (71.1 x 114.3)
The Regis Collection, Minneapolis

Sanford Tanks #2, 1939
Oil on canvas, 28 x 36 (71.1 x 91.4)
Private collection

Boiler Syntheses, 1942
Oil on canvas, 35¼ x 50¼ (89.5 x 127.6)
Munson-Williams-Proctor Institute Museum of Art,
  Utica

Grain Elevators from the Bridge, 1942
Oil on canvas, 50 x 40 (127 x 101.6)
Whitney Museum of American Art, New York;
  Gift of the Friends of the Whitney Museum of
  American Art   63.22

Bomber, 1944
Oil on canvas, 28 x 40 (71.1 x 101.6)

Aircraft Plant, 1945
Oil on canvas, 28 x 40 (71.1 x 101.6)
Cincinnati Art Museum; Gift of Emil Frank

Lights in an Aircraft Plant, 1945
Oil on canvas, 30⅜ x 40¼ (77.2 x 102.2)
National Gallery of Art, Washington, D.C.; Gift of
  Mr. and Mrs. Burton G. Tremaine

Test Able, 1946
Oil on canvas, 23⅝ x 17⅝ (60 x 44.8)
Georgia Museum of Art, The University of Georgia,
  Athens; Eva Underhill Holbrook Collection of
  American Art; Gift of Alfred H. Holbrook

Tour of Inspection, Bikini, 1946
Oil on canvas, 24 x 34 (61 x 86.4)

Factory with Yellow Center Shape, 1947
Oil on canvas, 28 x 40 (71.1 x 101.6)

Fisherman's Wharf, San Francisco, 1947–50
Oil on canvas, 30 x 40 (76.2 x 101.6)
Private collection

On the Sundeck, 1948
Oil on canvas, 30 x 45 (76.2 x 114.3)

Wharf Objects, Santa Barbara, 1948
Oil on canvas, 26 x 36 (66 x 91.4)
Collection of Paul J. Leaman, Jr.

Freight Cars, Minneapolis, 1949
Oil on canvas, 40 x 30 (101.6 x 76.2)
Collection of Wesley Love

Third Avenue Elevated, 1949
Oil on canvas, 29¾ x 40⅛ (75.6 x 101.9)
Walker Art Center, Minneapolis; Gift of the Gilbert
  M. Walker Fund

Boxcars, Minneapolis, 1949–52
Oil on canvas, 30 x 42 (76.2 x 106.7)

Boxcars, Minneapolis #2, 1949–61
Oil on canvas, 60 x 40 (152.4 x 101.6)

New Orleans Still Life, 1951
Oil on canvas, 30 x 45 (76.2 x 114.3)

First Avenue #1, 1953–54
Oil on canvas, 32 x 40 (81.3 x 101.6)

New Orleans #5, 1954
Oil on canvas, 50 x 36 (127 x 91.4)
Sheldon Memorial Art Gallery, University of
  Nebraska—Lincoln; F. M. Hall Collection

New Orleans #7, 1954–56
Oil on canvas, 40 x 28 (101.6 x 71.1)
The Lane Collection

Fishing Boats #5, 1956
Oil on canvas, 26¼ x 40 (66.7 x 101.6)
Private collection

Fishing Boats #6, 1956
Oil on canvas, 40 x 30 (101.6 x 76.2)

New Orleans #8, 1957–58
Oil on canvas, 28¾ x 21¼ (73 x 54)

New Orleans #9, 1957–58
Oil on canvas, 19¾ x 28¾ (50.2 x 73)

Construction #5, 1958
Oil on canvas, 36 x 26 (91.4 x 66)

Lobster Pots #3, 1960–63
Oil on canvas, 45 x 60 (114.3 x 152.4)

St. Gilles #1, 1962–63
Oil on canvas, 30 x 40 (76.2 x 101.6)

St. Gilles #4, 1962–63
Oil on canvas, 45 x 60 (114.3 x 152.4)

Port Clyde #1, c. 1965
Oil on canvas, 30¼ x 40¼ (76.8 x 102.7)
Collection of Mr. and Mrs. Graham Stafford

Torn Signs #2, 1967–68
Oil on canvas, 60¼ x 45¼ (153 x 114.9)
Hirshhorn Museum and Sculpture Garden,
  Smithsonian Institution, Washington, D.C.

Second Avenue Collage, 1969
Oil on canvas, 40 x 30 (101.6 x 76.2)

Seville, 1970
Oil on canvas, 36 x 50 (91.4 x 127)
Collection of Peggy Frank Crawford

Feeder Canal, Coulee Dam, 1971
Oil on canvas, 30¼ x 40⅞ (76.8 x 103.9)
Collection of Elaine and Henry Kaufman

Blue, Grey, Black, 1973
Oil on canvas, 50 x 36 (127 x 91.4)

Seville, At the Cathedral, 1974
Oil on canvas, 40 x 60 (101.6 x 152.4)

Hoover Dam, 1975
Oil on canvas, 40 x 30 (101.6 x 76.2)

Bora Bora II, 1975–76
Oil on canvas, 30 x 40 (76.2 x 101.6)

Seville, Semana Santa, 1975–76
Oil on canvas, 50 x 38 (127 x 96.5)

Drawings

Maitland Bridge, 1938
Pen and ink on paper, 5¾ x 7¼ (14.6 x 18.4)

Sanford Tanks, 1939
Watercolor on paper, 12¼ x 17 (31.1 x 43.2)

At the Dock #1, c. 1940
Watercolor on paper, 16 x 12 (40.6 x 30.5)
Collection of M. Vanderwoude

Boxcar, c. 1941
Watercolor on paper, 12 x 15⅞ (30.5 x 40.3)

Air Force Incident, 1944
Gouache on board, 11 x 8⅞ (27.9 x 22.5)

Lights in an Aircraft Plant, 1945
Gouache on paper, 10½ x 12 (26.7 x 30.5)
Collection of Christopher F. Middendorf

Mission #1, 1945
Pen and ink on paper, 14½ x 22½ (36.8 x 57.2)

Bomber, c. 1945
Gouache on board, 10½ x 15¼ (26.7 x 38.7)

Untitled (Aircraft Plant), c. 1945
Gouache on board, 10 x 14⅛ (25.4 x 35.9)

Untitled (Nudes), c. 1945
Pen and ink on paper, 10½ x 8½ (26.7 x 21.6)

Untitled (Plane Tail), c. 1945
Gouache and ink on paper, 10 x 15½ (25.4 x 39.8)

Wings, 1946
Gouache on board, 9 x 13 (22.9 x 33)

On the Sundeck, 1947
Pen and ink on paper, 11 x 14 (27.9 x 35.6)

Plane Forms with Light #2, 1947
Pen and ink on board, 9⅜ x 13¼ (23.8 x 33.7)
Collection of Robert Miller

Wharf Objects, 1947
Ink on paper, 11 x 14⅝ (27.9 x 37.1)
Collection of M. Vanderwoude

Boxcars, Minneapolis, 1948
Ink on paper, 7¼ x 10 (18.4 x 25.4)
Hirshhorn Estate

Fisherman's Wharf, San Francisco, 1948
Pen and ink on paper, 9½ x 14 (24.1 x 35.6)

Grain Elevators, c. 1948
Pen and ink on paper, 14½ x 11⅝ (36.8 x 29.5)

Untitled (Dock Objects), 1948
Pen and ink on paper, 8 x 11 (20.3 x 27.9)

Wharf Objects, 1948
Gouache on paper, 7 x 13 (17.8 x 33)
Collection of Peggy Frank Crawford

Wharf Objects #3, 1948
Gouache on paper, 9 x 13 (22.9 x 33)
Whitney Museum of American Art, New York;
    Promised gift of Jacqueline Fowler   P.1.85

Wharf Objects at Santa Barbara #2, 1948
Tempera on paper board, 15 x 22 (38.1 x 55.9)
Robert Miller Gallery, Inc., New York

Untitled (At the Dock), c. 1948
Pen and ink on paper, 6¾ x 10¼ (17.1 x 26)

Untitled (Third Avenue Elevated), c. 1949
Pen and ink on paper, 13½ x 10¼ (34.3 x 26)

Industrial Abstraction, 1940s
Gouache on board, 8½ x 14 (21.6 x 35.6)

Untitled (New Orleans Still Life), c. 1951
Pastel on paper, 13½ x 20½ (34.3 x 52.1)

Torn Signs, 1967
Pen and ink on paper, 11½ x 8¾ (29.2 x 22.2)

Los Penitentes, 1975
Brush and ink on paper, 13¾ x 21⅜ (34.9 x 54.3)

Seville, At the Cathedral, 1975
Watercolor on paper, 14 x 20¾ (35.6 x 52.7)

Prints

Red and Black, 1949
Silkscreen, 18¾ x 23¼ (47.6 x 59.1)

Wharf Objects at Santa Barbara, 1949
Etching, 9½ x 14⅛ (24.1 x 35.9)

Wharf Objects at Santa Barbara, 1949
Etching, 10¼ x 14¼ (26 x 36.2)

Cologne Landscape #6, 1951
Color lithograph, 14⅞ x 21⅛ (37.8 x 53.7)
Whitney Museum of American Art, New York;
    Gift of Charles Simon   71.77

Lifeboat Detail, 1951
Color lithograph, 10¼ x 16 (26 x 40.6)
Whitney Museum of American Art, New York;
    Gift of Charles Simon   71.115

Third Avenue Elevated #1, 1951
Color lithograph, 10⅜ x 17⁵⁄₁₆ (26.4 x 44)

Third Avenue Elevated #4, 1952
Color lithograph, 17⅛ x 10³⁄₁₆ (43.5 x 25.9)
Whitney Museum of American Art, New York;
    Gift of Charles Simon   71.145

Third Avenue Elevated #5, 1952
Lithograph, 17¼ x 10⅝ (43.8 x 27)
Whitney Museum of American Art, New York;
    Gift of Charles Simon   71.146

New Orleans #4, 1953
Lithograph, 26¼ x 19¼ (66.7 x 48.9)

Collage #5, 1955
Lithograph, 9 x 15¼ (22.9 x 38.7)
Whitney Museum of American Art, New York;
    Gift of Charles Simon   71.69

L'Étoile de L'Occident, 1955
Color lithograph, 10⅝ x 16¾ (27 x 42.5)
Whitney Museum of American Art, New York;
    Gift of Charles Simon   71.114

Freight Cars #2, 1955
Lithograph, 9⅞ x 14¼ (25.1 x 36.2)
Whitney Museum of American Art, New York;
    Gift of Charles Simon   71.95

The Glass #3, State III, 1955
Lithograph, 19¼ x 12½ (48.9 x 31.8)
Whitney Museum of American Art, New York;
    Gift of Charles Simon   71.100

The Glass #4, State I, 1955
Lithograph, 12⅝ x 19⅛ (32.1 x 48.6)
Whitney Museum of American Art, New York;
    Gift of Charles Simon   71.101

Nets (Croix de Vie), 1955
Color lithograph with gouache, 9¼ x 17 (23.5 x 43.2)

Croix de Vie, 1955–57
Lithograph, 10½ x 17½ (26.7 x 44.5)
Whitney Museum of American Art, New York;
    Gift of Charles Simon   71.86

New Orleans #8, 1957
Color lithograph, 19 x 11⅞ (48.3 x 30.2)
Whitney Museum of American Art, New York;
    Gift of Charles Simon   71.126

Toro Heads, 1957
Lithograph, 19¾ x 26 (50.2 x 66)
Whitney Museum of American Art, New York;
    Gift of Charles Simon   71.148

Toro with Cape, 1957
Lithograph, 14¾ x 21⅝ (37.5 x 54.9)
Whitney Museum of American Art, New York;
    Gift of Charles Simon   71.150

St. Gilles #2, 1962
Color lithograph, 17½ x 23⅞ (44.5 x 60.6)
Whitney Museum of American Art, New York;
    Gift of Charles Simon   71.135

At the Cathedral, State II, 1976
Etching and aquatint, 11⅝ x 8¾ (29.5 x 22.2)

Photographs

Gas Tanks, 1938
Silver gelatin print, 6 x 4⅜ (15.2 x 11.1)

Sanford Tanks, 1938
Silver gelatin print, 4⅝ x 6⅞ (11.7 x 17.5)

Untitled (Maitland Bridge), 1938
Eighteen silver gelatin prints, each approxim[ately]
2 x 2 (5.1 x 5.1)

Loading Grain, New Orleans, c. 1938
Silver gelatin print, 5¾ x 4⅜ (14.6 x 11.1)

Santa Barbara Wharf Objects, c. 1940
Silver gelatin print, 3¾ x 5½ (9.5 x 14)

Ship's Deck, 1946
Silver gelatin print, 5½ x 8½ (14 x 21.6)

Mackinaw-Oden, c. 1946
Silver gelatin print, 5¾ x 8½ (14.6 x 21.6)

Shadows on Boat Deck, 1947
Silver gelatin print, 6¼ x 9¼ (15.9 x 23.5)

Untitled (Ship's Vent), 1947
Silver gelatin print, 5¹¹⁄₁₆ x 8½ (14.1 x 21.6)

Boxcar, Minneapolis, 1948
Silver gelatin print, 6⅝ x 3⅜ (16.8 x 8.6)

Untitled (Mannequin in Store Window, New York City), c. 1948
Silver gelatin print, 6½ x 4½ (16.5 x 11.4)
J. Paul Getty Museum, Malibu

Third Avenue Elevated, 1949
Silver gelatin print, 13⁷⁄₁₆ x 9¹⁄₁₆ (34.1 x 23)

Third Avenue Elevated, Horizontal, 1949
Silver gelatin print, 6½ x 9½ (16.5 x 24.1)

Downtown Nightclub, New Orleans, 1950
Silver gelatin print, 10⅝ x 13⁹⁄₁₆ (27 x 34.4)

George Lewis, New Orleans, 1950
Silver gelatin print, 9⁹⁄₁₆ x 7¹¹⁄₁₆ (24.3 x 19.5)

Dancer at Dew Drop Inn, c. 1950
Silver gelatin print, 9½ x 7½ (24.1 x 19.1)

Dancer at Dew Drop Inn, La Salle, New Orleans, c. 1950
Silver gelatin print, 10 x 8 (25.4 x 20.3)
J. Paul Getty Museum, Malibu

Cologne, 1951
Silver gelatin print, 9 x 13 ⁷⁄₁₆ (22.9 x 34.1)

George Lewis' Mother, 1951
Silver gelatin print, 14 x 11 (35.6 x 27.9)

S.S. De Grasse, c. 1951
Silver gelatin print, 6¾ x 9½ (17.1 x 24.1)

Untitled (New Orleans Still Life), c. 1951
Silver gelatin print, 2½ x 3⁹⁄₁₆ (6.4 x 9)

Beauty Queens with Wine Glasses, 1952
Silver gelatin print, 6½ x 9½ (16.5 x 24.1)

Dancer at 500 Club, 1950s
Silver gelatin print, 9½ x 7¹¹⁄₁₆ (24.1 x 19.5)

Untitled (St. Louis Cemetery), 1950s
Silver gelatin print, 10¹¹⁄₁₆ x 11¹⁵⁄₁₆ (27.1 x 30.3)

Door of Pete and Jack's Barbershop, New Orleans, 1960
Silver gelatin print, 10 x 8 (25.4 x 20.3)
J. Paul Getty Museum, Malibu

Foil Covered Can with Handle, New Orleans Cemetery, 1960
Silver gelatin print, 10 x 8 (25.4 x 20.3)
J. Paul Getty Museum, Malibu

Untitled (Tony Almerico Orchestra), c. 1960
Silver gelatin print, 9⁹⁄₁₆ x 7¹¹⁄₁₆ (24.3 x 19.5)

Junk Cars, 1964
Silver gelatin print, 11 x 14 (27.9 x 35.6)
J. Paul Getty Museum, Malibu

Seville, 1967
Silver gelatin print, 13⁹⁄₁₆ x 9¼ (34.4 x 23.5)

Untitled (Shadows, Seville), 1967
Silver gelatin print, 9 x 13½ (22.9 x 34.3)

Transatlantic, Ship and Deck, 1968
Silver gelatin print, 9 x 13 (22.9 x 33)

Zetland, 1968
Silver gelatin print, 10 x 8 (25.4 x 20.3)
J. Paul Getty Museum, Malibu

Holder and Shadow, St. Louis Cemetery, New Orleans, 1969
Silver gelatin print, 9¾ x 7¾ (24.8 x 19.7)
J. Paul Getty Museum, Malibu

Coulee Dam Staging Area #2, 1971
Silver gelatin print, 9 x 13½ (22.9 x 34.3)

Penstock Leaves #1 (Coulee Dam), 1971
Silver gelatin print, 9¼ x 13⁹⁄₁₆ (23.5 x 34.4)

Lifeboat Propeller (Scotland), 1973
Silver gelatin print, 8 x 10 (20.3 x 25.4)

Untitled (New Orleans Cemetery), 1973
Silver gelatin print, 10⅜ x 10⁹⁄₁₆ (26.4 x 26.8)

Films

Various Depths, 1966
Black and white, 20 minutes

Big Bayou, Black, 1973
Black and white, 5 minutes

Room 333, 1973
Black and white, 5 minutes

Torn Signs, 1973
Black and white, 5 minutes

The River, 1974
Black and white, 22 minutes

Photograph Credits
The photographs reproduced have been supplied by the owners or custodians of the works of art, or, in the case of works belonging to the Ralston Crawford Estate, New York, were taken by Bill Jacobson, with the following exceptions:

David Allison: 34; Courtesy Edward L. Baldwin, Archivist, Lafayette High School Alumni Association, Buffalo: 1; Courtesy Cape Ann Historical Association, Gloucester: 2; Geoffrey Clements: 55, 116, 117, 119–21, 123; Robert Crawford: 19, 126; eeva-inkeri: 33, 138; Phillip Galgiani: 20; Helga Photo Studios, Inc.: 71; Michael McKelvey: 66; Scott Photographic Services: 68; Steven Sloman: 23, 28, 44, 59, 65, 105, 112.

This publication was organized at the Whitney Museum of American Art by Doris Palca, Head, Publications and Sales; Sheila Schwartz, Editor; Elaine Koss, Associate Editor; and Emily Russell Sussek, Secretary.

Designer: Michael Glass Design, Inc.
Typesetter: AnzoGraphics Computer Typographers
Printed in Japan by Toppan Printing Co.